GW00976199

THE PRIMARY HEAD

The Primary Head

PATRICK WHITAKER

HEINEMANN EDUCATIONAL BOOKS
LONDON

Heinemann Educational Books Ltd
22 Bedford Square, London WC1B 3HH
LONDON EDINBURGH MELBOURNE AUCKLAND
HONGKONG SINGAPORE KUALA LUMPUR NEW DELHI
IBADAN NAIROBI JOHANNESBURG
EXETER(NH) KINGSTON PORT OF SPAIN

© Patrick Whitaker 1983

First published 1983

British Library C.I.P. Data
Whitaker, Patrick
  The primary head.
  1. Elementary school principals — England
  I. Title
  372. 12'012'0942   LB2822.5

    ISBN 0 435 80917 2

Printed and bound in Great Britain by Biddles Ltd, Guildford.

Contents

To the memory of my mother and father

Go with the people,
Live among them,
Learn from them,
Love them,
Start with what they know,
Build on what they have.
Of the best leaders,
When their task is accomplished,
Their work done,
The people all remark
'We have done it ourselves'.

Ancient Taoist poem

Foreword

Almost all the books on management and administration of schools, and almost all the specialist courses available, are concerned with secondary, further, or higher education. Indeed, the first titles in this series were concerned with secondary schools. This has meant that there has been neither adequate support from detailed studies nor a bringing together of theory and practice for the heads and deputy heads of primary schools. With the simultaneous inclusion of two key titles — *Responsibility and Promotion in the Primary School* by Derek Waters and the present book, *The Primary Head* by Patrick Whitaker — the *Heinemann Organization in Schools Series* is redressing the balance.

It is clear from the HMI *Primary Survey* that leadership in primary schools is crucially important: the freedom of individual schools to shape their own structure, responsibility posts, curriculum, and relationship to the community is very great indeed despite the many constraints schools face. How best to seize the possibilities offered by that freedom is a challenge that has occupied primary heads over the years. Patrick Whitaker has had extensive teaching experience in primary schools and was a head for many years. He is now a local authority adviser for primary education. In this book he combines that experience with relevant organizational and management theory, drawing on the numerous studies of management in other sectors of education. The result is an analysis of primary school life securely based in reality together with suggestions for good practice. Both will be of great value to all heads and deputies in their search for ways of improving the quality of the education they offer.

Michael Marland

Preface

A great many books have been written about primary schools, but only in the last few years has the role of the headteacher come in for any serious consideration. Much of the literature of educational management is concerned with the secondary and tertiary stages, and an assumption seems to have developed that management considerations are not an important feature of the primary stage. That senior staff in primary schools have been slower to respond to the growing concern with organization and management factors is in some measure due to the fact that in primary schools it is more difficult to separate the management from the purely educational functions. Senior staff in secondary schools, with a higher proportion of non-teaching time, have had more opportunity to identify the management aspects of their roles and to develop the necessary expertise.

Many local authorities now offer courses for heads and deputies of primary schools, but the national pattern of preparation and training for headship is still somewhat haphazard. Undoubtedly the best training for headship should be experience as a deputy, but in too few cases do deputy heads find themselves fully involved in the management and leadership of their schools. This book is a contribution both to the training process itself and to the debate about how schools in the primary phase of education could and should be run. It is offered as a practical guide to the way a headteacher could go about the task of managing a primary school. It draws upon experience in two primary headships and involvement in conducting many courses on educational management.

In essence the book is about the headteacher's role in staff leadership and this implies that the ideas and strategies discussed have been developed with larger schools in mind. The advantage of the small primary school lies in its potential for greater informality of manage-

ment and easier communications. Some of the practical suggestions
made in the following chapters may seem out of place in very small
schools, yet while the details may need adapting to suit specific needs
and circumstances, the basic principles of leadership will remain the
same whatever the size of the institution.

Many people have contributed to the book, most indirectly and
some inadvertently. The colleagues who worked with me in my two
headships were very patient as I tested out my ideas, and their cooperation and enthusiasm I gratefully acknowledge. My pupils have taught
me that management skills emerge and develop very early in life and
that if only we would foster and encourage them throughout the
educational process there would be no need for management training
later.

Many teachers have attended my courses, challenged my views and
caused me to re-examine my assumptions. To them I owe a considerable debt of gratitude. To those who have given me so many opportunities to participate in programmes of in-service training I offer my
thanks.

My special and particular thanks to Michael Marland whose patient
help, advice and encouragement sustained me over the period of
writing; to my family for leaving me alone so that I could get on, and
for being there when I couldn't; and to Lesley Cooper for preparing
the manuscript.

Patrick Whitaker

1   Towards a Role Definition

Few people, I think, would challenge the notion that the schools of today are infinitely more complex organizations than they were twenty-five years ago. As the rate of social change has accelerated, so the role of the headteacher has become increasingly demanding. The trend towards the appointment of younger headteachers has broken the traditional assumption that headship is best prepared for by long service. Together with an increasing demand for training in headship has come the need to consider the role of the headteacher in a much more systematic way.

Much of the change related to the role of the headteacher stems from developments within the structure of our society. With the growth of the welfare state has come a much closer relationship with a variety of social and welfare agencies. Schools have had an important part to play in gradually increasing levels of care and protection afforded to children, so that not only has the relationship between the school, the home and the community become more apparent, it has also placed increasing responsibilities upon the participants in those relationships.

Putting aside the educational aspects of change, there are other reasons which have contributed to the altered role of the headteacher. An increase in the demand for public accountability has led to a tighter control over money spent. This in turn has put pressure on schools to give a higher priority than before to wise and careful distribution of resources. Perhaps what is most obvious is that the change process itself has involved growth and increase in the number and range of activities with which headteachers are expected to cope. Parents have come to play an increasingly important part in the life of the school, and while an improved partnership between parents and teachers is obviously beneficial to the educational process, heads and teachers now find that they are having to respond more consciously to higher and more vociferous parental expectation.

One of the problems for headteachers is how to manage this demand for accountability and how to construct an effective relationship with a public who do not seem at all sure what they want their education system to be. The number of pressure groups attempting to influence the way schools are run adds to the burden created by a polarized argument about whether primary schools are worse or better than they used to be. While hard and sometimes bitter questions are asked of the education system as a whole, it falls to individual headteachers to react on behalf of the schools for which they alone are responsible.

The report *Ten Good Schools* (DES 1977a) stated that a good head needs to be:

1   a public relations officer
2   a diplomat
3   a negotiator
4   a personnel manager.

Not at all the roles which tradition has associated with headship, although, of course, good heads have always demonstrated them. The point that headship needed some serious reconsideration was emphasized in the first key document of the 1970s 'Great Debate' — the government Green Paper *Education in Schools: A Consultative Document* (DES 1977b):

> . . . the continuing need for the training of senior teachers, especially heads of department and headteachers, for the complex tasks of school organization and management, including the design and planning of the curriculum, to help them make the most effective use of all available resources, not least the talents of the school staff itself, in providing for the diverse needs of their pupils.

Embodied within this statement is a clear recognition by central government that the roles and responsibilities of heads and senior staff have changed enormously in recent years. The Taylor Committee in their report *A New Partnership for Our Schools* (DES 1977c) recommended even wider and more radical changes. In an attempt to increase the level and degree of involvement of school governors with the running of schools, the committee made a number of proposals which, if implemented, would considerably increase the duties required of headteachers.

One of the fascinating paradoxes for new heads is the realization that while on the one hand they have great freedom to interpret their role as they wish, on the other hand what they do must in great measure match what is expected of them. Yet there is little contained in law, or the directives of local education authorities, to prescribe what a headteacher should do, a situation which contrasts strongly with the USA which has its state laws and district regulations for the organization and management of schools. Another curious paradox is that while primary schools represent wide differences of approach to the tasks of education, they also share fundamental similarities. Philosophies differ considerably, as do patterns of organization, but most primary schools subscribe to a basic half dozen subject areas. Clearly something beyond prescription is responsible for the pattern that has become established, and more particularly for the purposes of this book, why the role of the headteacher has developed as it has.

In attempting to answer this, it is necessary to examine the concept of role, and to try and piece together the various elements that combine to determine the work that a head does. When we talk about a role we are more concerned with the part played by an individual in social or organizational life, than with personality. The role a person is considered to be playing is, to a large extent, determined by a set of well-defined expectations. A teacher taking over the headship of a primary school will be aware of the traditions that have helped to develop the school to its present state and will also be conscious that associated with this new position are a set of functions the headteacher will be expected to perform.

In attempting to determine their own particular role, heads must have due regard for a whole range of factors which act together to influence their behaviour. These can be categorized as:

1 prescriptions
2 expectations
3 situations
4 predilections.

Let us examine these in turn.

1 Prescriptions

The 1944 Education Act which lays down the foundations of our post-war system of schooling has very little to say about the nature of headship. The only systematic attempt to define the role of the head is contained in the Rules of Government. All local education authorities in England and Wales issue Rules of Government for their primary schools. They are based on models sent out following the introduction of the 1944 Education Act. They were subject to revision following local government reorganization in 1974. Although there are local differences, the rules define the way a school shall be conducted, the procedure for appointing the staff, and determine the duties of the governors themselves, and also the head. The duties required of governors can be summarized as:

1   Inspection of school premises and keeping LEA informed of its condition and state of repair.
2   Appointment/dismissal of the headteacher.
3   Appointment/dismissal of teachers.
4   Appointment/dismissal of non-teaching staff.
5   General direction, in consultation with the headteacher, of the conduct and curriculum of the school.
6   Calling LEA's attention to any matter not in their power to control.
7   Full consultation at all times between the Chairman and the headteacher.
8   Granting of occasional holidays.

The Rules of Government prescribe the head's duties as: '. . . the headteacher shall control the internal organization, management and discipline of the school, shall exercise supervision over the teaching and non-teaching staff, and shall have the power of suspending pupils from attendance . . .'

It is clear that the governors are charged with considerable authority over the conduct and curriculum of the school and are accountable to the local education authority for a great deal of what goes on during the normal course of school events. The rules constantly emphasize the point that the running of the school is a joint enterprise between the governors and the head, as can be judged by the many references to the need for consultation. It was made very clear by Robin Auld QC in his report to the Inner London Education Authority on the public inquiry into the events at the William Tyndale Junior School (Auld 1976) that the failure to establish an adequate framework for consultation between the governors and the head and his staff was a crucial factor in the development of the unhappy and damaging situation at that school. This report is perhaps the best case study of school management that exists. The fact that what it reveals actually happened adds to its importance as an essential document for headship training.

Further prescriptions are contained in common law. These are essentially related to the child care aspect of school life and are to do with the head's duty to provide adequate supervision of pupils at all times. Headteachers also have considerable responsibilities under the Health and Safety at Work Act 1974, but at the time of writing the full implications of this are only just beginning to emerge and most LEAs are laying down clear and precise policies for the operation of these regulations. An essential handbook for all headteachers is *Teachers and the Law* by G. R. Barrell (1975).

An obvious place to look for further clues is in the head's contract of employment, but while this gives details of conditions of service and terms of employment it has virtually nothing to say about the work a headteacher should do.

Most heads receive a regular supply of memoranda, directives and procedures which are issued to schools by the local education authority. Most of these are to do with administrative matters and are designed to help make the local authority bureaucracy as efficient as possible. Many heads complain of the increasing burden of 'admin', and a common dilemma is how to carry out the purely educational and management responsibilities effectively, while at the same time coping with the quantity of paperwork which finds its way into the head's 'in-tray'.

2 Expectations

If it were possible to collect the public's views on the role of the head-teacher, it is likely they would include the following: 'to ensure the school prepares children adequately for life and work'; 'to run the school as a well-disciplined and organized community where children learn what is needed for future life'. While heads undoubtedly respond to such public expectations, they are also having to react to a wide variety of more specific demands both explicit and implied. Many heads spend a great deal of their time talking to parents about their child's attitudes, behaviour, relationships, health, eating habits and lost property, as well as their educational progress. Parents them-selves represent such a wide range of value positions on issues of disci-pline, behaviour, motivation, success and failure that no one school can hope to satisfy them all. While few headteachers would put the satisfying of parental wishes as their highest priority, most would acknowledge that they strive to run their schools to acceptable standards.

Assessing the nature and strength of local authority expectation is a much more difficult task. Perhaps the strongest control is exercised at the appointment stage. In fact it is in the pre-interview stage, the shortlisting of candidates for headship, that a local education author-ity begins to determine the qualities and skills that it hopes to find in those who will run its schools. Most primary heads are appointed by the traditional method whereby a shortlist is prepared from written applications and selected candidates are interviewed. It is worth looking at the advertisements for headships that are to be found in the educational press. The following are fairly typical:

Required for January, a headteacher with experience of modern teaching methods and working among children from multi-ethnic backgrounds, and with an awareness of community links.

Headteacher required. Appointment to take effect as soon as possible. This is an interesting and challenging post for an enthusiastic person. Applica-tion forms and further particulars . . . .

The vacancy arises from the promotion of the previous holder of the post, and it is hoped that the successful candidate will take up duty as from April, or earlier if possible. The post offers admirable scope for a teacher of energy and initiative.

Enthusiasm and energy seem to be the qualities that most LEAs prize, although it sometimes appears that availability is the strongest qualification of all. The further details on request rarely give any deeper indication of what the authority is looking for in its new head-teachers, consisting of information about the size of the school and design of the buildings. Although as yet there is little empirical research into the appointment system, the experience of many head-teachers seems to indicate that interviews follow a fairly common pattern, with questions on school organization, curriculum and methods of teaching occupying the majority of the time. In many authorities there is no one on the appointing panel who has had experience of primary headship, and it is not surprising that many LEAs regard a successful stint in the classroom and a few years in a deputy headship as sufficient qualification for the post of head. It is rare to come across a candidate whose leadership potential exercised the minds of the appointing body. If LEAs are to be successful in attracting applicants of high quality to their vacant headships, then both advertising and the provision of details need some rethinking. And if the best possible candidates are to be appointed, authorities must be prepared to spend more time and money on the selection procedure.

A distinct set of expectations, and considerably more subtle than those outlined above, are exercised by a new head's teaching col-leagues. A new head whose arrival is seen by colleagues as a threat to the status quo, will have a very different role from one who is welcomed as a prophet to lead colleagues to the promised land. Much will depend upon the personal and professional aspirations of the members of staff the head has to work with in determining the specific nature of the task.

3 Situations

Although a great many of the problems headteachers encounter are generic in nature, some relate to the specific situation of a particular school. Indeed, the whole question of situation is crucial in the selec-tion of the headteacher, and of staff. Part of the selection procedure should be to relate the qualities and aptitudes of the candidate to the specific requirements of the school. In attempting to replace the head-teacher of a school which has been very well run for a number of years, and which needs a period of consolidation following curriculum change, it might be unwise to select the candidate whose chief quality is a proven capacity for vigorous innovation. Consideration of the following list of vacant headship situations will demonstrate the range that does exist:

1 New school: basic need.
2 New school: replacement of old accommodation with new open-plan building.
3 Reorganized school: amalgamation of an infant and junior school on the same site.
4 Extended school: additions due to closure of smaller local schools.
5 Reducing school: declining numbers on roll resulting in reduced staff, classes and removal of temporary buildings.
6 Split site: local authority plans for replacement postponed because of lack of finance.
7 Star school: used by the authority as a show school.
8 Good school: well-organized, high staff and pupil morale, clear policies and high standards.
9 Steady school: traditional organization, curriculum and teaching style, but good standards and parental confidence.
10 Confused school: poor leadership has failed to overcome problems of variable teaching style, no coherent policies and variable standards.
11 Unhappy school: low staff and pupil morale, anxious and complaining parents.
12 'At risk' school: poor learning environment combined with lack of leadership and coordination. Regarded by LEA as a problem.

Most local authorities will have schools conforming to these rather subjective descriptions but they do emphasize how important it is for potential headship candidates to know something of a school's successes and failures, its problems and needs, as well as the nature of the building, the number on roll and its Burnham grouping. As we shall see in the next chapter, part of a new head's task is a systematic analysis of the school, but this should not be an alternative to a prior insight into the key features of the school and its performance. Presumably the applicant for a chief executive post in an industrial organization would have the opportunity to study the balance sheet of a company before agreeing to take on its leadership. Local authorities will not get the best out of their new heads if they fail to alert them to the difficulties a school is experiencing as well as to its more positive aspects. At the very least candidates for interview should have a thorough briefing by senior officers of the authority when specific difficulties can be described in some detail and something of the LEA's expectations of the new head declared. Following appointment the head elect should further be taken into the confidence of the LEA and the school's governing body.

4 Predilections

There must be room in any role definition for an individual's aspirations. Most teachers arrive in headship determined to avoid the glaring errors they have witnessed in heads they have worked with, but also equally determined to bring to reality some long cherished visions of the way a school should be run. Again, selection for headship should take into account the applicant's hopes and aspirations. Certainly a great deal more could be made of the written application as a vital source of important information. Application forms are invariably for biographical and professional experience details and it is left to the candidate to stake a claim in a supporting letter. Good applicants are those who best anticipate what it is the selectors want to know, and what is likely to impress them most. Would it not be more sensible to suggest items or questions to which candidates should respond in their letter? The list would vary according to the nature of the school and the particular professional qualities being sought. Far too many questions asked in the brief interview that headship candidates are given could more easily be dealt with at the application stage. Part of the interview could then profitably be devoted to following-up responses to these key points.

However, headship is not an opportunity for self indulgence and a school is a complex organization to which a new head has to adapt with skill and understanding. Other members of staff will have their cherished visions too and these will deserve attention and consideration.

Defining the role

In coming to terms with the role a new head is faced with something of a balancing act. To the collection of tasks that must be done, and those that are expected to be done, must be added those which the particular school situation demands; only then can the head see what space is left for those he or she would like to do. It should be clear by now that a variety of factors influence the way a headteacher goes about the tasks. In the end it is the head who will formulate a role which is both acceptable and manageable.

A most interesting insight into how primary school heads perceived their role was given in *The Headteacher's Role* (Cook and Mack 1971). The following list represents the range of tasks and duties that head-teachers considered most important:

  Having a clearly defined policy
  Building a team of competent teachers
  Facilitating the professional development of teachers
  Establishing good personal relationships

Being seen as a good teacher
Resolving conflict
Keeping up to date on educational developments
Introducing new ideas
Administering and maintaining the organization
Appointing staff
Knowing the children
Evaluating the work of the school.

Any leadership role in an organization grows and develops according to trends and circumstances. To avoid falling into the trap of simply responding to problems as they arise, it is best to begin a new headship with some clear idea of how the job is to be tackled. In undertaking a role-defining exercise the head is not attempting to create a straight-jacket, but trying to come to a precise understanding of the nature of the responsibilities, in order to select from the range of activities with which heads are traditionally concerned, those specific tasks which are relevant to the particular situation.

In *School Decision-Making* Cyril Poster (1976) provides an excellent set of considerations for defining a role (see Fig. 1.1, below). This clearly divides the definition into two distinct halves: one to do with the nature of the responsibility inherent in the role, and the other with decision-making. In terms of responsibility the head is faced with four questions:

1 For whom am I responsible?
2 To whom am I responsible?

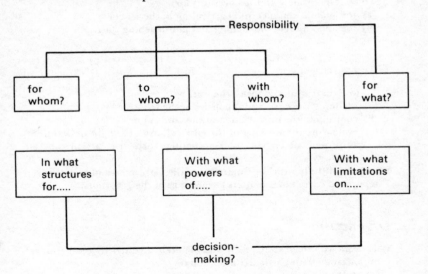

Figure 1.1   Considerations in constructing role definition

3 With whom am I responsible?
4 For what am I responsible?

The role definition will be of little use if it fails to answer these questions. Before the content of the role definition can be determined it is
necessary to consider its design. Poster strongly urges that it should not
simply be a list of duties. This would allow little room for manoeuvre,
inhibit initiative and encourage conformity. In a profession, it is
essential for the details of the role to be developed by the individual.
What is required is a clear indication of the nature of the job.
Recalling the heads prescriptive duty to 'control the internal organization, management and discipline of the school' we are provided with
an outline. This can undergo further elaboration until the definition is
complete. By way of example the following role definition for a head
of a primary school attempts to answer the questions asked earlier, and
also to relate activities to various structures within the school.

Role definition

Authority and responsibility

1 To be responsible to the governors for:
   (a) the internal organization, management and discipline of the school
   (b) the supervision of the teaching and non-teaching staff.
2 To be responsible with the governors for:
   (a) the general conduct and curriculum of the school
   (b) the appointment of teaching and non-teaching staff.

Curriculum

1 To work in consultation with the staff on:
   (a) planning the curriculum policies of the school
   (b) controlling the organization of the curriculum
   (c) evaluating the working of the curriculum in the light of planned
       aims and objectives, and initiating corrective action where
       necessary.
2 To consult fully with the Chairman of the Governors and to submit
   reports on curriculum matters to meetings of the governors.

Organization

1 To work with the staff to create and maintain an efficient and happy
   organization with particular attention to:
   (a) staffing
   (b) distribution of finance and resources

(c) supervision of pupils.
2 To create and maintain a decision-making structure providing facilities for participation by the staff.
3 To create and maintain an efficient system of communication.

People

1 Through the exercise of a teaching role to get to know as many children as possible.
2 To have regular contacts with all members of the teaching and non-teaching staff.
3 To help, support and advise staff in the pursuit of their duties and the development of their careers.
4 To be available to:
(a) children
(b) teachers
(c) non-teaching staff
(d) governors
(e) parents
(f) LEA officials
(g) HMI
(h) visitors.

This should not be regarded as a definitive statement, but rather as a model from which to depart. For some it will be too specific, while for others it will not say enough. Whatever form it takes it will serve no purpose if it is locked away in a drawer and forgotten. It is best used as a reminder of the theoretical perceptions of the job, to be considered in relation to the actual activities that occupy the head's time. If there is a wide gap between the theory and the reality then either something is wrong with the role definition, or the head is very inefficient. It is not too uncommon to hear heads complain that they never get round to doing their 'real' work. Efficiency can only begin when the nature of the job in hand has been clearly formulated and a determination to stick to it established. One answer to those who complain of being deviated from their intentions is a more strenuous effort to plan their work. For some, the gap between intention and action is almost unbridgeable, but it need not be. Stated simply the problem is solved by knowing what needs doing and allocating time to do it. Quite the best book I have read on this subject is *The Effective Executive* (Drucker 1967) which is full of wise and practical advice for the inefficient, and even has words of comfort for those who have difficulty organizing their desk. In Drucker's view the only way to deal with an apparently unmanageable workload is to 'do first things first and second things not at all'.

Pursuing the role

A clear role definition is only the first step towards efficient headship. Following the commitment to paper of the role definition there arises the question of what to do with it. Certainly it should be shared with certain key people. Advisers and senior officers should be invited to comment upon it. The chairperson of governors should have a copy and the new head will wish to refer to it when speaking to the governing body of plans for the development of the school. A later chapter will discuss job descriptions in some detail when the point will be made that all such documents should be in the possession of each member of staff. I can think of no valid reason why a new head should not want colleagues to know how he or she sees the new role.

There is no denying the real frustrations of constantly having to deal with the urgent at the expense of the important. The following strategy may go some way to help. Planning work is essentially a matter of setting targets, breaking the time available for dealing with them into manageable units and allocating time as accurately as possible. There are four stages linking the overall conception of the job with the performance of individual tasks:

1   *Role definition*: outlining the job in hand for the foreseeable future.
2   *Year plan*: a set of aims to be achieved by the end of the academic year.
3   *Term plan*: a list of precise objectives for the term.
4   *Action programme*: the tasks and activities necessary to accomplish the term's objectives.

A head who is under a lot of pressure may find it helpful, and necessary, to take this strategy some stages further. For example, it is useful to devote the last hour of the working week to planning the next week's programme. This is an excellent habit to cultivate at the end of each working day. In fact it is very important when planning work to include time for planning future work. It should go without saying that establishment of orderly working habits such as a tidy desk, efficient storage of papers, good telephone technique together with a calm disposition, are essential if the head is to serve the school efficiently and successfully.

References

AULD, R. (1976) *William Tyndale Junior and Infant Schools Public Inquiry* London: ILEA
BARRELL, G.R. (1975) *Teachers and the Law* London: Methuen

COOK, A and MACK, H. (1971) *The Headteacher's Role* London: Macmillan

DES (1977a) *Ten Good Schools: A Secondary School Enquiry* London: HMSO

DES (1977b) *Education in Schools: A Consultative Document* Command 6869 London: HMSO

DES (1977c) *A New Partnership for Our Schools* (The Taylor Report) London: HMSO

DRUCKER, P.F. (1967) *The Effective Excutive* London: Heinemann

POSTER, C.D. (1976) *School Decision-Making: Educational Management in Secondary Schools* London: Heinemann Educational.

2 Taking Over

The process of taking over really starts at the moment the appointment is offered and accepted. If it is a first appointment, speculation will centre on the nature of headship itself, and if a second or third headship, thinking will probably reflect a determination to synthesize previous headship experience. However, the aftermath of an interview is no time to start making plans for the future and it is usually with some sense of relief that the new appointee makes farewells and seeks out some solitude in which to contemplate this significant event.

Preparing for the takeover

After the promotional euphoria has begun to wear off, and the business of resignation has been dealt with, a sense of ambivalence is likely, since it is necessary to serve out one post and at the same time look forward with some expectation to the one that is to come. Undoubtedly there will be an eagerness to become immersed in the new experience of headship, but it will be wise to regard the weeks before taking up the new post as a period of preparation. This new job is going to make quite different demands and although the full significance of these cannot be anticipated, it is as well to be ready for the rigours ahead. The demands of the new job are most likely to make their presence felt in the challenge to intellectual capacity and practical competence, two qualities the appointing board should have been looking for. Therefore, in this time before taking up the new post some thought and consideration should be given to these two areas, and since practical competence tends to develop with experience, attention must first be focused on the intellectual challenge of the job.

The interval between the interview and taking up the appointment

is an unreal time in that preparation for the post cannot adequately
take account of the essential ingredient of good decision-making — a
thorough knowledge of the school. However, some time can probably
be devoted to theoretical notions of education in general, and primary
schooling in particular. The emphasis of this thinking should not be
on answers and solutions but on the questions posed by the prospect of
headship.

What are the aims of primary education?
How can they best be expressed?
What form should the curriculum take?
What are the advantages — disadvantages of the various forms of
    class groupings?
What are the merits of various teaching styles?
What is an appropriate learning environment for children of
    primary age?
What sort of social order should a primary school have?

To some extent answers to such questions as these will have been
rehearsed for the interview. Now they take on an altogether more
profound purpose. While it is essential to retain an open mind about
the best practical solutions to them, it is important for the head elect to
have given deep thought to the fundamental issues of primary school
education. Our system of education allows for the development of
many different approaches to teaching and the running of schools;
what it should not tolerate is any approach that is not the result of deep
thinking and conscious choice.

On the practical side of preparation for the takeover, a programme
of visits to the school should be undertaken. The main objective of this
will be to help make the transition from one head to another as smooth
as possible, with the minimum of disruption to the school. It is unlikely
that a new head will be taking over directly from a predecessor, unless
the latter's resignation is due to retirement. Because of the length of
notice required for heads to resign their post there is usually a
complete term between one head leaving and another taking over. It is
usual for an acting head to be running the school during the transi-
tional term, and in most situations the deputy head will assume this
role. Being an acting head obviously gives a deputy valuable experience in actually running a school, but because of its transitory nature
it can be a difficult role to fulfil. Usually the acting head will be only
too pleased to consult with the future head on major developments
and will welcome the opportunity to discuss various issues as they arise.
It is usual, for example, for heads to be involved in any appointments
that have to be made during the term leading up to the takeover.

A visit to the school during this transition period will serve a number
of purposes. First, it will be an opportunity to get to know the various
people who make up the school organization. The new head can be

formally introduced to any members of staff not already met, and will have a chance to further relationships previously established. Perhaps for the first time there will be an opportunity to meet the children. They will be no less curious than the staff to see what the new head is like, and they will be anxious to know what the head thinks of them. Second, the visit will present the opportunity to test out theories. The fundamental question foremost in the new head's mind will be about how closely this organization comes to satisfying his or her own views of how a school should be run. The impressions which are gained during the visit will provide further food for thought during the time leading up to the takeover. Third, there will be essential management and administrative matters to discuss with the acting head. These may include important matters of finance, staff deployment, resource allocation or appointments. Fourth, these discussions will be the starting point for the most vital of relationships, that between the head and the deputy. It is essential that these two key figures establish a good working relationship from the start and this is probably best achieved by the new head looking to the deputy for guidance during the early period of the new régime. Certainly there will be many occasions during the first term when the new head will wish to seek the sort of advice that can best be provided by an able deputy who has been in the school for some time. What the new head should avoid in these visits is creating an impression of trying to run things before actually taking over.

Other sorts of visit are sometimes arranged for the head elect — an invitation to join the school governors' termly meeting, an opportunity to speak at a meeting of parents, or perhaps more informally at a social occasion. While it is important not to overdo these contacts, a few well planned visits will serve to prepare the way for an easy and efficient takeover.

Newly-appointed heads are likely to approach the new job with a mixture of pleasure and uncertainty. There is pleasure in the prospect of having the opportunity to do those things they have always felt they could do given half a chance; and uncertainty about how those they are called upon to lead will react to their plans. Having been selected from many colleagues in open competition it will be difficult to submerge the sense of mission that inevitably accompanies the prospect of entry into a new headship.

For some new heads this sense of mission takes the form of an overriding determination to put into operation as quickly as possible those educational philosophies that have laid dormant for so long. For others, personal esteem and professional respect are more valued currency than educational ideology, and for them the prime task is to establish good relationships and create conditions of mutual trust. Some others perhaps approach their new jobs with no fixed notion of what they will do or how they will do it.

What is certain however is that the newly-appointed head will be anxious to make a good start. The first few days in office will be very important. The new head will be under scrutiny from the start, and first impressions can sometimes be very powerful indicators of character and personality.

The takeover

The final stage of preparation will occur in the holiday before the takeover. Apart from coming to terms with the geography of the building, the most important act of preparation is that of the new head's own place of work. Unlike conditions in the civil service, head-teachers' offices conform to no predetermined pattern of design or furnishing. Much will depend upon the age of the school and anything can be expected from a sumptuous executive suite to a pokey cup-board. More than a few heads have to satisfy themselves with a garden shed in the playground. But whatever its size and the quality of its furnishings the office will have to serve a number of purposes. First, it must be a place where the head can talk in privacy to colleagues, parents or visitors. I can see no virtue in extending the open-plan concept to include staffrooms and offices. There are times when private conversations have to be held with no fear of being overheard, and there must be a place in the school where this can happen. Second, it is a place where visitors are entertained and, third, it is a place where the head does some of his or her work.

What heads do with their office and how they use it is again very much a matter of personal preference. In one school I know it is affec-tionately referred to as 'the greenhouse', while in another it is very much 'the nerve centre'. A great deal will depend upon the sort of management style that is to be adopted and the extent to which the head is seen as a fellow colleague on the teaching staff. The head's office should be well organized and tidy with seating available for callers whether they be children, colleagues or parents. There should be some attempt to reflect the life of the school with children's work on display rather than timetables and duty rotas. When arranging the office the head has to consider how other people are to regard it, and what is to be the rule about access. A permanently open door certainly makes for easy access and communication, whereas a policy of perma-nent closure tends to inhibit what may be casual but important visits from staff and children. Perhaps one of the best approaches, condi-tions of comfort allowing, is only to have the door closed when it is important not to be disturbed. Most heads would be anxious to avoid the jibe about being 'always in the office'.

The first day in any new job is important, perhaps for a new head it is doubly so. Not only will some thought have been given to what to wear but also to what time to arrive. Everyone will have their own view on both these points but it will be unwise to establish too early a reputation for bizarre behaviour like the new head who wore a totally different form of dress each day of the week in order to try and find out which one made the most impact upon staff. As for time of arrival, some heads like to be there first and busy at work by the time the rest of the staff and the children arrive, while others prefer a more flexible approach. What soon becomes evident is that the ten or fifteen minutes before the school day officially starts is a time of concentrated decision-making, with absent staff to be covered, early phone calls to be dealt with and often parents to be seen.

Apart from these preliminary considerations perhaps the most important thing for the head to decide about the first day is what he or she will actually do. A great deal obviously depends upon the amount of contact there has been with the school. If visits have already been made and the head has met all new colleagues, and perhaps the children too, then the first day need pose no great problems. What is important is to make contact with all members of staff, teaching and non-teaching, as early in the day as possible. This is a good routine to establish and it will convey the fact that one of the head's prime considerations is the welfare and well-being of the staff.

Perhaps the most important impression to create on the first day is that of being actively involved in the life of the school by visiting colleagues in their classrooms preparing for the day ahead, talking to the children as they come into school, making contact with parents as they deposit their infant children on the premises. A tour of the site and buildings with the caretaker will be an early priority in view of responsibilities under the Health and Safety at Work Act. A visit to the school kitchen is also important.

The first assembly as head of the school will be a telling occasion. It is through this daily meeting of the whole school, which should include non-teaching staff whenever possible, that the head exercises influence over the corporate life of the organization. By the choice of themes, music, words and objects the head should strive to create an atmosphere in which each child and adult can relate their own inner life to that of the school as a whole. This first occasion will need more preparation than most. It should not be too ambitious, nor too long, but sow some of the seeds from which the new leadership will grow.

A key member of the school staff is the clerical assistant and it is important for the new head to take an early opportunity to discuss the essential routines and procedures of the school. Unless it is made clear by the new head how they are to work together, the clerical assistant is likely to continue the procedures approved by the previous head. Even quite mundane issues need resolving, such as

1   who answers the telephone?
2   who opens the post?
3   who deals with routine visitors/inquiries?

4   who signs the forms?
5   who has access to the filing cabinets?

A competent and efficient clerical assistant, given sufficient hours, can undertake a wide range of work which is often undertaken by heads themselves. This is the one role in the school which the new head needs to get right early on. It is not a question of increasing the clerical assistant's work load but of agreeing together what the priorities of the job are.

Before their first day is over most new heads will have begun to draw up a balance sheet. On one side will be those aspects of school life of which the head approves, and on the other, less satisfactory aspects. According to the state of this balance sheet there will already be emerging some obvious areas where changes will need to be made. In fact by lunchtime on the first day new heads will probably have made a number of changes simply because their personalities differ from those of their predecessors. While it is unlikely that they will have begun to influence the formal structures of the school, their arrival will have had some impact upon the informal structures. In personal contacts with staff or children, or perhaps by the nature and content of the first assembly the head may have done things which a predecessor would never have dreamt of doing. Whether this balance sheet exists only vaguely in the new head's mind or has actually been committed to paper it will be obvious that those factors which occupy the debit side do so because they are quite obviously at variance with the rationally-held theory of education that has already been referred to. This will present the first management dilemma. The head will be aware, in theory at least, that the staff are keyed up to expect some changes to be made, and will also be aware of the dangers of acting too soon before there has been time to examine issues in some detail. The dilemma is that a head who moves too quickly may mistakenly decide to change policy, one who delays too long could miss the opportunity of undertaking change at a time when the staff are most receptive to it.

This brings back the question of management style and approach. One new head after his first week in a long-established primary school called a staff meeting, handed to each teacher a set of papers and said, 'From now on I want things done this way,' and went on to outline his new system for running the school set out in the papers. In contrasting style another head also called a staff meeting after a week or so, but this time said to those assembled, 'I've had a good look round the school and everything seems to be in order.' With that he retired to his room and was rarely seen again. Extreme examples perhaps, but I suspect there are more than a few teachers who would recognize either of those brief descriptions. Since this whole book is concerned with the business of management style and strategies for running a primary school, it will be necessary to get to the end before the beginning of the process can be seen in its true perspective. But a start has to be made

somewhere and the following outline is offered first since it is a strategy
which needs to be undertaken very soon after a new head takes up the
post.

Taking stock

If lucky, the first few days in office can be comparatively calm for a
new head. Most matters to be dealt with will be of a fairly routine
nature, and there should be some opportunity to begin the first major
task of headship — accumulating the information necessary to determine the course of action to be taken. There is a tendency to decide on
courses of action on incomplete or even false evidence, and if this
mistake is to be avoided the process of information gathering will need
to be painstaking and thorough.

One of the most vital skills a head needs is that of accurate analysis
— to be able to see where the real problems lie, and to be able to dis-
criminate between what is fundamental and what is only of minor
importance. Sound analysis is at the heart of good decision-making
and it is a skill worthy of cultivation.

The process of analysis undertaken at the beginning of a new headship is concerned with gaining a clear and complete perspective of the
school and how it functions. Essentially this fact-gathering process is
about finding answers to a number of questions:

1   What goes on in this organization?
2   What are its chief features and characteristics?
3   What needs to be done?

These and many such similar questions need detailed and complete
answers before the head is in any position to contemplate initiating
change. This taking stock operation is designed to provide all the
information needed to build policy, make plans and decide on a
course of action.

The new head will have gathered some information from pre-
appointment visits to the school — impressions of how the school
goes about its work, what sort of social order it enjoys, and perhaps
something about the teaching styles of the various members of staff. In
addition the head may well have decided what sort of challenge this
job is going to be and whether it will involve major tasks of reorganization or mere corrections of course; or alternatively may have considered the chances of achieving the sort of school he or she would
dearly like to be identified with. But just as new heads would not wish
to be judged by the earliest impressions they make, so too must they be
determined not to evaluate the school too hastily.

In this data-gathering process it is important to distinguish between
facts and impressions, particularly if the information is to be used as
the basis for future decision-making. There are various ways of classi-

fying the information upon which analysis will be based. One method would be to make a list of all the factors about the school the head needs information on. Another way would be to research each class at a time. While the second approach is somewhat more systematic, neither is likely to reveal the essential and complete information that is being sought.

An analytical exercise of this nature should be based on clear objectives. From the general aim of gaining a clear and complete perspective of the school a list of precise objectives can be derived. It is here that an organizational model can be so helpful. The school can be regarded as having three distinctive but interrelated elements:

1 *Curriculum dimension*: the formal and informal learning structures of the school.
2 *Social dimension*: the structures arising out of the relationships between individuals and groups within the school.

Analysis checklist − *curriculum dimension*

Ref.	Information required	Source	Date
1	*Written statements*		
a	Aims and objectives		
b	Curriculum statements		
c	Syllabuses		
d	Schemes of work		
2	*Records*		
a	Central files		
b	Records on children		
c	Teachers' records of work done		
d	Pupil progress		
3	*The timetable*		
4	*Resources*		
a	Reading		
b	English		
c	Mathematics		
d	Humanities		
e	Music		
f	Art/Craft		
g	PE		
5	*Evaluation*		
a	Tests		
b	Reports		

3   *Organizational dimension*: the structures that bring order, and establish procedures for the efficient running of the school.

As well as proving useful in the solving of organizational problems such a model can facilitate the very process of analysis itself. For each of the model's three dimensions an analytical checklist can be designed. That on page 21 is offered as an example and is by no means exhaustive.

Similar checklists in the other dimensions can be developed. For the purpose of analysis each of these dimensions could be further subdivided, and precisely how this is done would depend upon the nature of the head's particular educational theories. A useful example of how analysis can be affected by educational theory is the way the problem of class organization is tackled in different primary schools. Given a three-form entry junior school, four approaches to this problem come readily to mind:

School A
1st year   [A] [B] [C]
2nd year   [A] [B] [C]
3rd year   [A] [B] [C]
4th year   [A] [B] [C]

School B
1st year   [M] [M] [M]
2nd year   [M] [M] [M]
3rd year   [M] [M] [M]
4th year   [M] [M] [M]

School C
1st year
2nd year
3rd year
4th year

School D
1st year
2nd year
3rd year
4th year

School A
Children are allocated to classes on the basis of age and ability. Each year-group will have three classes and they will be streamed according to ability

School B
In this school there is no streaming but children are placed according to age. In each year-group there will be three parallel mixed-ability classes.

School C
Here partial vertical-grouping has been adopted. There is a division into lower and upper juniors, each having six parallel vertically-grouped classes.

School D
Team-teaching and vertical-grouping have been adopted. There are three fully vertically-grouped teams.

Clearly, four examples cannot represent the whole variety of approaches employed by British primary schools. But from the brief descriptions it is not difficult to imagine how different the approach to the curriculum would be in each of the schools. Those who have chosen to organize their schools on the basis of streamed year-groups do so for their own deeply-felt reasons, and the same assumption must be made for those who adopt a different organizational pattern. A new head who believed in streamed year-groups would have no major conflict to face if appointed to School A in the example above. But if the same head were appointed to School D it might lead to something of a predicament.

In facing up to these issues it will be important for the head to resist the temptation to interpret evidence solely on the basis of preferred practice. In determining the effectiveness of the way the classes are organized it is not enough to look only at the way children are distributed between teachers; there must also be evidence that this particular form of organization facilitates the learning process. If, during the analysis process, the head discovers practices that conflict with particular personal theories, then the problem is what to do about it. Initially the most important task will be to submit to re-examination the assumptions upon which the head's theories are based.

During the writing of this chapter an incident occurred which will serve as an interesting illustration of the point just made. A group of deputy heads were looking around a school which employed vertical-grouping in its junior classes. The deputy of the school who was acting as guide to the group was asked how the school justified vertical-grouping in a school of its size. The teacher who asked the question worked in a school where all classes were based on horizontal-groupings and could not understand why any school would adopt a vertical organization from choice rather than necessity. The worrying point about this illustration is that the visiting deputy had wrongly assumed that given a choice everybody would want to do things his way.

During the analysis of the school the head will certainly be making many value judgements about the work that is going on. What must be guarded against are the assumptions which ultimately rely on the belief of the infallibility of the head's theories. In cultivating ideological tolerance a head needs to become familiar with sets of assumptions that guide those who hold different theories.

Collecting information

Basically there are three methods of collecting information for analysis.

1   Personal observation

It is only by becoming thoroughly immersed in the work of the school that heads are likely to get to know what really goes on. They will need to draw upon their experience as class teachers to appreciate fully and understand the various teaching methods that are employed. By witnessing at first hand the activities that children are engaged in they will slowly build a picture of the organization at work. Whatever other methods heads employ it is personal observation and involvement that will prove to be the most reliable means of determining what the school is trying to do, how it goes about it and how successful it is.

Children are only likely to behave naturally in the presence of the head who is a familiar figure around the school. Heads who are always in their office can never hope to know what goes on, and their rare appearances will probably have the human telegraph wires humming. So, for this personal observation to be vaild, the head's presence around the school needs to become a natural and accepted part of activities.

2   Informal contacts

A wealth of information can be accumulated from informal contacts. Conversations with children are likely to provide the new head with a revealing insight into the school and it would be wise to take advantage of such contacts as often as possible. The sort of head/staff relationships which emerge are very much a personal consideration, but whatever leadership style is adopted both head and staff stand to gain if such relationships are relaxed and supportive. Informal contacts with the non-teaching staff are particularly important, as their contribution to school life can often be undervalued and pass unnoticed. Through conversations with colleagues, the head will begin to discover something of the complex web of attitudes and opinions that are so characteristic of organizations, and will gradually come to recognize and understand the human forces at work, and the nature of personal and group interaction. It is essential to get this part of the exercise right, for if the wrong assumptions are made about the people in the organization, then the tasks of management and leadership are likely to be very fraught.

3 Formal methods

Some work will need to be done on a formal basis. If the school has been open for some years it will probably have accumulated a hefty collection of documents. As well as children's records there will be other documents such as the school log-book and the proceedings of governors' meetings. Files of correspondence, memoranda and forms can prove both interesting and informative, and a journey through the filing cabinets should be an early priority. Some documents of course are more likely to provide an insight into the recent history of the school than an exposition of its present state of being, and providing this is understood it is all relevant to this process. Even the way that files and documents are ordered and maintained will say something about the school and the way it has been run.

Some heads fight shy of formal contacts with members of staff. By these are meant interviews formally arranged and with a specific purpose in mind. There are a number of benefits to be derived from such meetings, some of which will be discussed in a later chapter, but in the initial process of analysis the formal interview provides the head with the opportunity to meet each member of staff and talk about his or her part in the life of the school. The purposes of such meetings should be known to all and arrangements made well in advance.

Another formal method of gathering information is the questionnaire. If used wisely, and not too often, this is a useful device when responses to specific plans or problems are required. The benefits are twofold. First, the questionnaire can obtain the view of everyone involved in an impersonal way, since the responses are not subject to justification in discussion. Second, they can be so designed as to provide a reasonably reliable guide to the way members of staff feel about an issue. Matters of confidentiality and anonymity need to be made clear however if the results of such a technique are to be valid.

Staff meetings can be a source of useful information about personal and group dynamics.

Certain members of staff can play a key part in providing information. The deputy head whose knowledge and guidance are likely to be in considerable demand, has a particularly important role to play in helping the head to settle into the new job. The caretaker and the kitchen staff can prove useful indicators of the school's social order, and the secretary is usually a fount of knowledge with the particular understanding of the school that her role brings.

Having decided what information to collect and how to go about obtaining it, some thought needs to be given to the question of what to do with it. A great deal will be stored in the memory, but undoubtedly it will be necessary to keep some record. The analysis checklists can be designed in such a way as to facilitiate this. When a particular item of information is obtained the checklist can be ticked off and the reference number attached to any papers to facilitate orderly storage and future reference. If considerable documentation is undertaken, separate files for the various subject areas will probably prove helpful.

The end-product of this information-collecting process will be the analysis itself. This is where decisions about the information are taken. If future developments in the school are to be properly evaluated it is essential that some sort of report is prepared. Even if this report is no more than a personal memorandum it will serve a most useful purpose, for not only will it be the obvious consequence of an important management function, but in future years it will stand as a reminder of the way the school was when it was taken over. It is surprising how quickly this, and all the progress that has been made, can be forgotten.

The report need not be lengthy. In essence it is a collection of statements about the school based on the information that has been collected. These statements will form the basis of the new head's formulation of policy, general aims, and specific and immediate objectives. From an analysis of the human forces at work in the school organization the head will determine the style of leadership that is likely to prove the most effective in the realization of those aims.

Once again making use of the organizational model, the table of contents for the report could well be:

1   Title of report
2   Building and site
3   Personnel
    (a) teaching staff
    (b) non-teaching staff
4   Curriculum dimension
    (a) Content
    (b) Teaching methods
    (c) Evaluation and assessment
5   Social dimension
    (a) School rules
    (b) Relationships
    (c) Attitudes of care
6   Organizational dimension
    (a) Responsibilities of staff
    (b) Timetable arrangements
    (c) Consultative process
    (d) Decision-making procedure
    (e) Communications
7   External relationships
    (a) Parents
    (b) Community
    (c) LEA
    (d) Other schools
8   Summary and conclusions
    (a) Curriculum dimension
    (b) Social dimension
    (c) Organizational dimension

It is in section 8 of the report that evaluation of the preceding statements is made. The conclusions themselves are really a declaration of where the head stands in relation to what has been inherited, and an indication of the policies which will be pursued. The preparation of this analytical report is the new head's fundamental task after getting to know the staff. Not only will it provide a clear perspective in which to view possible future developments, but it will also serve to indicate what room for manoeuvre there is likely to be in the pursuit of aims.

Reference

DRUCKER, P.F. (1967) *The Effective Executive* London: Heinemann

3   A Question of Style

While a great deal of attention is focused on what headteachers should do, not enough consideration is given to how they should do it. Yet it is the manner in which heads go about their work, rather than the nature of the tasks themselves, which determines the degree of success.

Definitions of leadership abound. The working definition I will adopt is that of leadership as the influencing of group activity in determining what needs to be done, how it is done and if it has been successful. It implies the creating and maintaining of relationships of trust, and the development of mutual dependence among members of staff.

It is crucial for the head to appreciate that a school is a human organization established for the specific purpose of achieving certain agreed aims, and to understand that the fundamental leadership task is to make the two elements — people and purpose — compatible. The possibility of succeeding in this will to a large extent depend upon heads' capacity to understand the people they work with, and to reconcile their individual and perhaps conflicting aims with those of the school as a whole. Heads work through and with people, and must therefore give thought to the way individuals and groups interact in an organizational setting. Whether this understanding is achieved by the somewhat academic route through the literature of organization theory, or as is more likely, through a healthy curiosity about why people behave in the way they do, matters only to the individual. In the end experience will be the most formative influence in helping to avoid repeating the mistakes that inevitably will be made.

Some teachers enter headship with a confident prediction that the school will soon bend to their ways. More perhaps approach it with a sense of dread that certain firmly-held beliefs about the way schools should be run will be compromised. Headteachers have to recognize that the nature of their task is to a great extent determined by the organization they are to lead. This requires the development of a sensitivity to personal and group interaction, and some grasp of the behaviour patterns within organizations.

In the leadership capacity within the school organization the head has two main concerns — the people he or she works with, and the tasks they are there to carry out. It is these two functions which featured first in the role definition. This can be shown diagramatically:

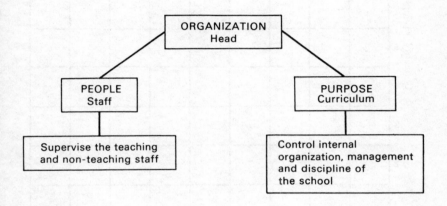

Figure 3.1   Organization: people and purpose

An interesting theoretical device which explains this idea and relates it to leadership style is the managerial grid (see Fig. 3.2, p. 30) designed by Robert Blake and Jane Mouton (1971).

The grid represents eighty-one potential leadership styles. Only five of these are described in the text and a most interesting and useful exercise is to attempt a description of them all and then to try and rank them in some order of priority. Despite its simplicity the grid will repay study.

Translating this to headship we have:

1.1   This head has little concern for either the educational purposes of the school or the staff and children, and complains of being weighed down with paper work.

9.1   This type of head has an overwhelming concern for high standards of work from teachers and children. He or she is autocratic, makes the decisions and expects them to be carried out, and expects the school to bend to his or her wishes.

1.9   Blake and Mouton call this 'country club management' and it typifies the head who takes the view that the school is only as

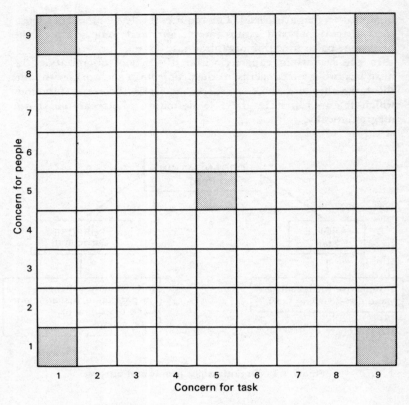

Figure 3.2   The Management Grid

good as its teachers can make it. Such a head is casual and informal and tends to gloss over problems in the hope that they will go away. Happiness of the pupils is seen as the main indicator of effective learning.

5.5   This type of head tries to achieve the happy medium and in doing so fails to satisfy the requirements of either.

9.9   This is regarded as the model to strive for. A high concern for people is matched with a high concern for the tasks the school has set itself. This style of leadership begins with the assumption that the two elements can be satisfactorily combined, and works to the principle that the personal identification of each member with the aims and objectives of the school and their related tasks can bring about high morale which is an indicator of a dynamic and flourishing organization. High regard is attached to team-work, and conflict is recognized not as something to be avoided at all costs, but as an essential ingredient of the corporate process.

In this consideration of leadership it is interesting to speculate on the particular qualities that appointing panels are looking for in potential heads. The technique would seem to be to try to see which of the half dozen or so candidates has the most complete blend of personality, confidence and determination. One member of an appointing panel once asked a female candidate, 'Can you handle men?' A familiar question asks the candidate to explain how to deal with a difficult member of staff. These and other questions like them fail to understand the true nature of leadership, which is not about having stock answers for stock situations, but of having the ability to understand a situation and to adapt behaviour accordingly. Most heads have been led to believe that the qualities they already possess are the ones that will serve them best. But this is not always so, and a vital quality of leadership is the capacity to recognize weaknesses and work towards their removal, as well as to foster strengths.

It needs to be stressed that corporate leadership in the primary school is not a means whereby the head can ease the burden of responsibility. If anything, responsibility increases, and good leadership will involve the head's willingness to relinquish some authority through a process of delegation, while at the same time continuing to accept responsibility for all that goes on. In order to achieve the right conditions in which such a style of leadership can flourish some attention to the structure of the process will be necessary. All the staff will need to be very clear about:

1 *Roles*: their own particularly, but also those of all other staff.
2 *School philosophy*: teamwork depends upon a strong personal identity with the goals the school is aiming for and anything less than a thorough familiarity with the aims, policies and procedures of the school will inhibit its achievement.
3 *Decision-making*: how decisions are made, who is involved and at what stage. Unless everyone is familiar with the procedures for initiating the decision-making process, tension will be created and teamwork will suffer.
4 *Evaluation*: relating results to intentions is an essential part of the process and everyone needs to know if they as individuals are succeeding, and whether the corporate venture of which they are part is achieving its goals.

Creating good teamwork takes time and involves change within a school. Not only is it necessary to establish and maintain good supporting structures, but also to be aware of the nature and extent of individual and personal changes that result. The greater the consensus of individual values, then the more tightly knit is the corporate identity, the feeling of being a united staff, a successful team. But this may only come about following a process of development for each individual member. Teachers familiar only with fairly autocratic leadership may

feel somewhat insecure when invited to participate in a more democratic approach to the running of the school. The sorts of personal
changes that may be necessary can be considered under four headings:

1 *Skills*
Essentially these are the skills concerned with inter-personal communication. In a successful team there is an increased capacity to accept
the validity of other people's points of view, and a determination to
recognize the common ground while at the same time preserving an
essential element of autonomy. Teachers in open-plan schools find
this, and it can take a considerable measure of adjustment until new
skills are developed, previous working habits modified and more
tolerant attitudes established.

2 *Confidence*
A dynamic group derives its collective strength from the ability of
individuals to work confidently using their strengths while openly
admitting their weaknesses. Confidence will grow as new skills develop
and succeed. The head has an especially important role to play in
helping colleagues to adjust to a new situation, and needs to be sensitive to the inevitable tensions that will arise from time to time.

3 *Initiative*
As individual skills develop and confidence grows, the working group
will become more cohesive, more open and more ready to join in discussion about its progress. By fostering the development of strengths
and talents in colleagues, the head will also be encouraging a positive
and dynamic involvement in group decision-making. If individual
proposals and suggestions receive fair and sympathetic consideration,
then initiative will grow and flourish.

4 *Responsibility*
Eventually individuals will respond to an increasing group morale by
showing a greater willingness to accept a larger share of responsibility
for the corporate venture. In a flourishing and healthy group there is
a positive thirst for responsibility as individuals begin to enjoy the
greater satisfactions that accompany this way of working.

I am aware that I have made the transformation to dynamic teamwork seem a very simple process. That it can never be, and in attempting to create the necessary conditions for corporate leadership the
head will encounter many obstacles and receive countless disappoint-
ments, but that is in the nature of the job. Some heads may feel a
natural affinity with a style of leadership which involves a distribution
of power and authority amongst the staff, but given the conditions
that exist in their schools cannot imagine how it could be achieved.
High teacher turnover, low staff morale or a preponderance of young
and inexperienced teachers can appear as overwhelming constraints.
Change should be regarded in evolutionary rather than revolutionary
terms, as a process of steady development during which new structures
are gradually introduced and assimilated. Much will depend upon
headteachers' ability to understand the effect of change on colleagues,

and their regard for staff welfare and well being.

Many attempts have been made to isolate management skills and even to rank them in importance. The following six functions offer the beginnings of a framework:

1 *Planning*
   (a) relating present to future needs
   (b) recognizing what is important and what is merely urgent
   (c) seeing ahead
   (d) anticipating future trends
   (e) analysing
2 *Creating*
   (a) having good ideas
   (b) finding original solutions to common problems
   (c) anticipating the consequences of decisions and actions
3 *Communicating*
   (a) understanding people
   (b) listening
   (c) explaining
   (d) getting others to talk
   (e) tact
   (f) tolerance of others' mistakes
   (g) giving honest praise and honest criticism
   (h) keeping everyone who needs to be informed.
4 *Controlling*
   (a) comparing outcomes with plans
   (b) self evaluation
   (c) evaluating the work of others
   (d) taking corrective action where necessary.
5 *Motivating*
   (a) inspiring others
   (b) providing realistic challenges
   (c) helping others to set themselves realistic and challenging targets
   (d) helping others to value their own worth.
6 *Organizing*
   (a) making fair demands on people
   (b) making rapid decisions
   (c) being in front when it counts
   (d) staying calm when the going is difficult
   (e) recognizing when the job is done.

Heads will vary considerably in the competence with which they will exercise these skills, and indeed the many others that are not included in the list.

No consideration of leadership would be complete without some attention to the question of authority and power as it affects the head's position. By title the head is singled out as the most senior teacher, and under the arrangements of the Burnham Committee is paid on a different salary scale – an added recognition of status and responsibility. There is some argument as to whether headteachers are paid more because of the nature of their work, or because they alone are finally accountable for what goes on in the school. The following are fairly typical comments made about headteachers: 'Heads have too much power and not enough accountability'; 'The head's authority is constantly being challenged'; 'The head alone should not be expected to cope with the vastly increased responsibility he or she has to carry'. These conflicting views reveal something of the confusion over terms such as 'authority' and 'power' and it is important to try and unravel them.

The authority of the head is as much a matter of tradition as of precept. Society has become accustomed to the idea that heads run their schools, and the education system supports this notion. Through the Rules of Government the position and status of headteachers is acknowledged. Through a process of delegation coming down from central government, through the local education authorities and the governors, headteachers receive their authority. This gives them the right to carry out the duties commensurate with the job, but whether or not they are able to do this will depend upon their power. In *The Sociology of the School* Marten Shipman (1968) considers the parts that authority and power play in the relationship between pupil and teacher. I quote this here because a similar situation exists in the relationship between the head and the other teachers on the staff:

> The difference between power and authority is crucial . . . power, the ability to get obedience, can be a barrier in education unless it is accepted voluntarily. . . . Education is impossible if obedience has to be imposed. Only when children grant the teachers the right to exercise power can they exert their full academic and moral influence.

I am not suggesting that the relationship between pupils and teachers is at all similar to that between teachers and the head, but that the *nature* of power and authority is similar. While authority gives heads a right to 'control the internal organization, management and discipline of the school', it is their power which is the force that sees that it is done. Yet in the school situation it is power which is granted, which is recognized as legitimate. In most work situations power hinges on a system of rewards and punishment, rewards in terms of remuneration for work done, and punishment in terms of dismissal from the job. In these particular areas heads have very little power indeed. It is true they are able to recommend payment beyond the limited structure of the Burnham Committee rules, but where extra allowances have been allocated the head has no power to remove them. The authority to make appointments to the teaching staff lies with the governors, although in most cases they are made through a process of consultation. So in terms of 'hiring and firing' heads have virtually no power at all.

Responsibility, another key concept within this context, can be defined as the obligation to do something. As such it is a quality inherent in the individual and not imposed from without. It is the way that a person responds to authority delegated from a senior colleague. Accountability on the other hand is the duty to give account to that senior colleague, or a superior, for the work that the delegated authority demands. In the primary school situation the sense of responsibility will vary from teacher to teacher whereas accountability can be prescribed within a role definition.

The relationship between the head and staff is formally structured through the system of authority and power, yet organizations cannot flourish on such arbitrary concepts alone. There is a good deal more to headship then defining authority and attempting to exercise power. If the head is to be successful in leading the school towards the achievement of its agreed aims there has to be some measure of consensus. The means of achieving the desired aims have to win the general approval of those who will do the work. Such consensus is achieved more by influence and persuasion, as a careful study of Blake and Mouton's managerial grid will reveal (see Fig. 3.2, p. 30).

There are three distinct ways in which the head can exercise leadership. First, as a colleague, available to share with staff the day-to-day problems of running the school, by participating in group discussions, reflecting on the problems of individual children with a class teacher, or perhaps teaching. Here the head will be exercising leadership in an unobtrusive and informal way.

Second, there will be times when the head will need to act as a guide, feeding in new ideas, defining and explaining school philosophy to new members of staff, or assisting with specific problems. In this capacity a head may be the initiator of a programme of school-based in-service training and from time to time may act as an adviser on career and promotion questions.

Third, there will be times when a lead is required and the only place for the head to be is out in front. When the going is hard or morale is sagging a clear initiative may serve to ease the apparent burdens of a situation. There will be occasions when the head will have to represent colleagues and to speak up on their behalf. Good leadership implies an infinite capacity for absorbing knocks, and being in front when it counts wins loyalty as surely as delegating blame loses it.

Headship is not just about getting things done, of taking the school in a personally predetermined direction, nor of taking it as far as circumstances would seem to permit. Rather it is about creating the right conditions in which the staff as a whole can share the vision of what is possible and work together for its realization.

High on the list of headship qualities is the ability to understand people and to work with and through them. Since the first of those abilities must precede the second it is important for the head to develop an adequate capacity to analyse the nature of human interaction within the school. It is not simply a case of being good at recognizing strengths and weaknesses in teachers, but of being able to answer the deeper questions of why people behave in the way they do. On the basis of this understanding the head will then be able to proceed to an anticipation of how individuals will react to praise, criticism or suggestions for change. Attempting to understand human nature and behaviour is a daunting occupation full of hazards and pitfalls, but successful leaders get their results by being good at it. By cultivating organizational awareness, by being tuned in to the human forces that so affect the day-to-day running of a school, the head should be able to anticipate the likely outcomes of his or her own behaviour. There are no short cuts to the acquisition of such understanding, but the head who chooses to ignore the importance of mutually trusting relationships does so at peril.

In Chapter 2 it was suggested that a new head would need to give some thought to this question of relationships with colleagues. Thinking again of the managerial grid it will be fairly obvious that the different styles of leadership are founded on different sorts of relationships. The two extremes are the formality and distance cultivated by the autocratic head, and the over familiar 'one of the boys' approach of Blake and Mouton's 'country club' style.

In striving to establish the corporate model it will be necessary to develop the sorts of relationships that result in mutual trust and understanding. True teamwork requires a high degree of integration between leader and team, and if there are to be frank and honest exchanges of view between all the participants then some informality is desirable. Kindly manners and consideration may sometimes be found to be counter-productive but should never be sacrificed. As to the use of first names, that is a matter for individuals to decide. The prime consideration is the promotion of mutual trust, the breaking down of unnecessary barriers between people and the development of a sense of interdependence.

Tension is sometimes created by the fact that the head spends too much time in the staffroom. Better that, I think, than a head who is an isolated figure unwilling to relax with colleagues and join them in the lighter moments of school life. It is not possible to be a 'boss' and truly one of the boys, and the exercise is not worth the effort. However much of a team member the head may be, there will be occasions when the staff will want to be on their own.

Part of the head's skill is gauging the nature and degree of interaction to have with staff — getting it right will depend upon a high degree of sensitivity to group and individual feelings. The fact is, of course, that these are not always compatible and the head needs to be good at knowing when to try and ease tension and when to leave it well alone. The deputy has a crucial role in this respect and it is just these qualities that the head should be encouraging and fostering. All situations that arise in the school are vital case studies for the professional development of both head and deputy.

Leadership in the school situation has an endemic frustration. Unlike participants in other kinds of institution the staff of a primary school are with the children for the greater part of their working day, and breaks and lunchtimes are often the only occasions when the head can make contact with colleagues, either individually or collectively. Consequently, communication is difficult to maintain and many of the frustrations of working in a primary school, particularly where teamwork is practised, can be attributed to poor and inadequate communication. The head needs to give some priority to being available, but also needs to make a point of establishing regular contact with each member of staff, both teaching and non-teaching. In a small or medium-sized school this can be a daily routine, but in larger schools some imagination needs to be applied if the head is to avoid becoming too remote from the rest of the team.

Heads stand or fall by the quality of their communication and nothing is more likely to create tension among a team than lack of information. Fig. 3.3 attempts to illustrate a communications

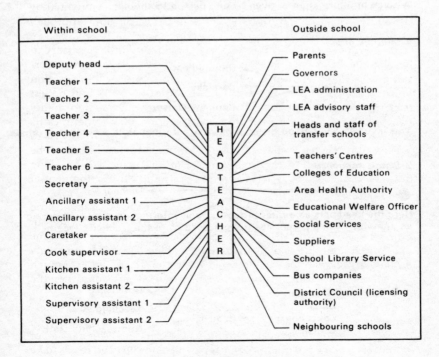

Figure 3.3   A communications network

network for a school of about 200 children. In the interests of simplicity the children of the school have not been included in the diagram but are, of course, very much a key feature of the network.

Clearly headteachers have no choice but to be the nerve centre of the network situated as they are at the centre of their own internal organization and also as the link between the school and the outside world. During the normal course of a school day it is usually only the head who is available to deal with the communication tasks that inevitably arise. It is a most revealing exercise to record communication tasks for a school week and to analyse how much time was devoted to dealing with issues arising from them. There is much that a good secretary can do to release the head from many of these tasks, but as the staffing situation in primary schools makes it very unlikely that other members of staff have non-teaching roles, then it is the head who must bear the brunt of this work.

There are various types of communication tasks with which the head is involved:

1 *Simple direct*

Head ⟶ Deputy head

A piece of information is given by one person to another.

2 *Multiple direct*

This involves one person giving a piece of information to a number of others.

3 *Simple sequence*

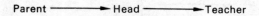

Here the head acts as a filter process. Some information conveyed during an interview with a parent has to be passed on to the teacher concerned.

4 *Multiple sequence*

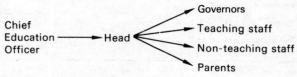

Again the head acts as a filter process.

5 *Simple reciprocal*

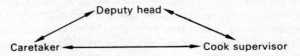

Here the head and the deputy are in a communicating relationship. They will probably meet daily to share new information and to bring each other up to date on current issues and activities.

6 *Multiple reciprocal*

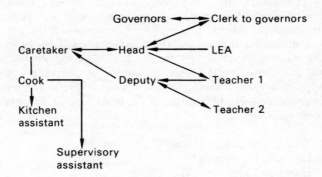

In this situation a number of people are involved. If the participants are together at the same time then it becomes a meeting.

7 *Network*

Governors ←→ Clerk to governors

Caretaker ←→ Head ← LEA

Cook ——— Deputy ← Teacher 1

Kitchen assistant

Supervisory assistant

Teacher 2

A network contains all examples. Although a school of 200 children is a comparatively small organization, the communications network that it represents will defy precise definition, and this is some indication of the complexity of organizational life. The creation and maintenance of an adequate communication system is an awesome task for the head, particularly as the more dynamic the organization becomes the greater is the demand for information, and the greater the sense of frustration when the system cannot match up to the new demands being made upon it.

The communication system of a school can be regarded as having three essential elements:

1   official communications procedures
2   the 'grapevine'
3   personal communication factors.

The school's official procedures will include all the deliberate devices to facilitate quick and easy communications. These will range from the complex patterns of decision-making to the apparently simple technique of posting notices on a board. Formal procedures for conveying information and dealing with messages need to be discussed and documented. All members of staff need to be aware of their own responsibility to help maintain the system in a healthy state. Failures and breakdowns need to be considered so that they can be avoided in future.

In organizations where the official system is in a poor state, the 'grapevine' takes over. If members of staff are deprived of information they will tend to invent their own, and the existence of rumour is some indicator of success with the official system. However, the 'grapevine' is an important element of any communications system and although less accurate is certainly quicker.

The success of a communications system is dependent upon the communication skills of the individuals operating it. If the head is a poor communicator, it is likely that the system will inhibit the development of good teamwork. Questions of how, where and when information is conveyed are of crucial importance. Bad communications lead to confusion, misinterpretation and consequently inefficiency.

Communicating is one of the vital functions of headship, and one of the most difficult to get right. It needs considerable effort, and adequate time, for it is only by painstaking planning and meticulous application that the vital organizational lifelines can be maintained. Some success will be ensured if the head constantly seeks answers to these questions:

Who ought to know what?
How will they get to know?
How will I know that they know?

References

BLAKE, R.R. and MOUTON, J.S. (1971) in D.S. Pugh, D.J. Hickson, C.R. Hinings (eds) *Writers on Organizations* Harmondsworth: Penguin
SHIPMAN, M. (1968) *The Sociology of the School* London: Longman

4   The Decision-making Process

Although teachers are taking decisions all the time, those that a head is faced with have a different feel about them altogether. Within the school it is the head who has the highest authority to take decisions affecting what goes on, and the sobering realization that headship also involves accepting responsibility for all decisions taken is not slow in dawning. It is this realization that urges some heads to inhibit both teachers and children in the way they go about their work in the school by insisting on having the last word even on quite petty matters.

There is considerable difference between 'decision-taking,' and 'decision-making'. In the normal run of school life the former is an event − a question is asked and an answer is given. Decision-making on the other hand is a process in which the taking of decisions plays only a part, and it is with this process that this chapter is concerned.

The purpose of decision-making in school is to maintain a dynamic momentum. It is part of a cyclic process in which the results of earlier decisions create the needs for new ones to be made. It is also the process by which the school responds to newly recognized needs. The reason that decision-making attracts so much attention these days is that the increasing rate of change in society that organizations have to respond to, is forcing schools to examine emerging needs more regularly than before.

Two distinct types of need are relevant. First there are the needs that emerge from within the school itself, which will be specific. They will include the content and design of the curriculum, the way in which children are distributed among the teachers, and the particular scale posts held by individual teachers. Second, there are a range of general needs which are identified through means external to the school.

One of the great challenges of headship these days is deciding how to respond to the many and varied pronouncements that are made about the way primary schools are run, and what they should be doing. For most heads, facing up to the internal problems of the school is challenge enough, having to react to the relentless demands from outside the school as well, is only serving to increase the professional dilemma in which many heads find themselves. One of the extra roles that heads are now having to exercise is that of relating the findings of surveys and reports to their own school situations. Too much of this and there is a danger that attention will be diverted from more pressing local needs.

A strategy which attempts to keep these two elements in proportion has to be developed. Chapter 1 stressed how important it was for the head to have a clearly-formulated philosophy of education, and public pronouncements, if regarded as challenges and not threats, provide an opportunity to submit to re-examination those aspects of educational philosophy under consideration. Such a strategy is one which sets out to reconcile the needs of individuals with those of the school as a whole, and it calls upon the qualities of leadership which were the subject of the previous chapter.

One of the key themes of this book is that many of the activities traditionally undertaken by the head alone are really the concern of every teacher. The style of leadership recommended is one which views each individual member of staff as a participant in the organization and management of the school, and which places their welfare and professional development amongst the head's most important responsibilities.

It is not my intention to try and impose upon the informal and intimate structure of the primary school a set of techniques that will result in over-organization, increased bureaucracy or an overt concern for 'management'. That management techniques have a vital role in the running of a primary school I have no doubt, and they are included in this book where they are relevant to the educational purposes the school is concerned with, and if children feature little in these pages it is because it is with their teachers that I am most concerned. Yet constantly in the forefront of my mind is the desire to make schools interesting and exciting places for children.

From the vision to the reality can be a large step; what goes on between is the question concerning most heads. To move from the present to a more desirable future involves changes, some fundamental and all embracing, others subtle and barely perceptible. The decision-making process is a sequence of events which handles these changes in a thorough and systematic way. It is a process which has equal applicability to minor routine issues as it does to matters of major importance. If the head's decision-making role is to be carried out consistently well a basic procedure needs to be adopted. Such a procedure will need to be simple enough to be acquired as a routine, yet sufficiently rigorous to embody all aspects of even the most complex issue.

Using a medical analogy, the core ingredients of any decision-making can be described as:

1 diagnosing the complaint
2 deciding the cure
3 administering the treatment.

In other words something is found to be wrong and a solution is found and implemented. Expanding this to acknowledge the precise stages involved we have a decision-making process containing six main elements:

1 recognizing the problem
2 analysing the problem
3 working out alternative solutions
4 choosing the best alternative
5 implementing the chosen solution
6 evaluating its effectiveness.

1 Recognizing the problem

The decision-making process is only brought into play if there is a need for something to change, if there is a problem. In a primary school it is usually only the head who is in a position to take an overall view, to see the school as more than a combination of its parts. Consequently it is likely that many of the problems submitted to the decision-making process will be done so on the head's initiative. Class teachers on the other hand are best able to identify specific curriculum problems, either in terms of standards of work, or of curriculum design and content. This is especially true where they have special responsibility for a curriculum area.

Such issues will enter the decision-making process following discussions between individuals and the head, or perhaps as the result of more general staff discussion. In a school run on autocratic lines, staff initiatives are not encouraged; but in a well-integrated and cohesive team there is little reluctance on the part of individuals or groups to bring matters of importance to the attention of the head.

Outside pressures have already been mentioned, but the following example will serve to emphasize the way that external influences can affect decision-making in schools. In September 1978 *Primary Education in England: A Survey by HM Inspectors of Schools* (DES 1978) was published. Among its comments on the curriculum was the following statement about science:

Few primary schools visited in the course of this survey had effective programmes for the teaching of science. There was a lack of appropriate equipment; insufficient attention was given to ensuring proper coverage of key scientific notions; the teaching of processes and skills such as observing, formulating hypotheses, experimenting and recording was often superficial. The work in observational and experimental science was less well matched to children's capabilities than work in any other area of the curriculum.

Such was professional sensitivity to these observations that by the end of that autumn term many LEAs had set up extra in-service courses on the teaching of science and publishers' representatives were promising a new wave of material that would help schools to cope with this 'new' problem. Some schools will have responded by sending teachers on the courses, or by undertaking an examination of this particular curriculum area. On the other hand, one school I know of, conscious that the comments by HMI could have been aimed directly at its own attempts to do some science, refused to be deviated from a current plan to improve the quality of art in the school.

The taking stock exercise discussed in Chapter 2 will have resulted in the identification of a range of issues which the new head feels require some attention, and an attempt to indicate priorities. Eventually problems will become identified as the result of evaluating the innovations, but that is some time away, the early years of a new headship will be a process of readjustment from the previous leadership to the new one.

2 Analysis

There is a danger that some issues can be regarded as problems when none exist. This is sometimes the case early in a new headship when what the school is doing does not match the head's preferred way of doing it. It is important to guard against a tendency to assume that the use of unfamiliar equipment, or non-favoured textbooks, will result in children receiving an inferior education. A bad day in the classroom or a poor set of results can sometimes bring about a feeling that something basic is wrong and needs changing.

This second stage of the process is a vitally important one for it involves a detailed examination of the problem area. The initial question is − what evidence is there that a problem exists? In order to be systematic and thorough in following-up superficial evidence, it is necessary to have some device to ensure that all avenues are explored. The analysis checklist described in Chapter 2 could act as a useful guide in determining the aspects to be considered, but since different kinds of problems require separate and individual analysis, a checklist specially designed for the purpose would be more suitable. Careful documentation of all stages of the decision-making process is to be recommended, and it is helpful to have to hand specially printed forms. In completing a form such as this the head, or anyone else who is undertaking the task, will be listing specific aspects of the problem which require investigation. These fall under two headings: factual data, usually in the form of documents and correspondence; and opinions and views. The form once completed serves as a checklist of tasks to be undertaken.

A situation arose in one school where the head and a new Scale 2 teacher, Miss Sinclair, had taken up their posts at the same time. The new head had not been involved in Miss Sinclair's appointment. The following extract from the head's notes outlines a problem that arose:

1   Ted Day has confronted me twice about Jane Sinclair's Scale 2 post (mathematics). Ted has maths as part of a composite Scale 2 portfolio and wonders what the situation is.

2   Deputy reports that few of the staff are aware of each others' areas of responsibility and Ted has spoken in some anger to DH about his conflict with Jane. Apparently she wants to undo some of the initiatives that Ted has made over the past two years.

3   Spoke to Jane. She was not aware that Ted had any responsibility for maths. Certainly she was not informed about it when she accepted the post and discussed her responsibilities with the previous head. She is now unhappy about the confusion and consequent bad feeling that has been created.

Using this situation let us see how the analysis checklist might be used to facilitate an investigation of the problem.

Date   *Analysis of*: Posts of responsibility

Brief statement of problem: A growing sense of role conflict among scale post-holders. Evident lack of knowledge.

People to consult: 1 DH
                                2 All post-holders, i.e. AMH, JS, ED, AJP
                                3 Clerk to governors
                                4 Chairman

Check the following:
1 List of scale posts
2 Any role definitions?
3 Correspondence re appointment/promotions
4 Appointment forms
5 See each post-holder — verify their own individual role conception: AMH; JS; ED; AJP.
6 Relate posts to aims of school
7 How were nature of responsibilities previously decided?
8 If role definitions were clear and generally known, would each individual be happy with theirs?

A further aid to analysis, and indeed to many other areas of decision-making, is the use of a conceptual model of the school. Such models attempt to portray the reality of a situation in visual form and if well constructed can deepen understanding of the situation and reveal fresh insights about it. Such models, or intellectual maps, are more commonly used than might be expected as John Holt reveals in this brief extract from *Freedom and Beyond* (Holt 1973): 'Like the economist, the traffic engineer, the social planner, or the computer expert, children at play often make models of life or certain parts of life, models they hope are fair, if simpler representations of the world, so that by working these models they may attain some idea of how the world works or might work or what they might do in it.'

Good models portray with great economy ideas that can take many words to explain. One example of a familiar model employed by most schools is the timetable which displays in diagramatic form the way that learning activities are organized. As Holt suggests there is much to be gained through the construction of such devices. Although in themselves models do nothing to improve the efficiency of a school, or to make the job of the head any less demanding, they can help to increase understanding of how the school works and so improve the insights that inform its decisions.

The analysis process needs to be planned in some detail. Fig. 4.1 (p. 47) suggests the stages to be followed.

If many staff are involved it will be necessary to lay down guidelines on coordination and timing. An action plan either posted on the staff noticeboard or given to each member of staff will help to keep things on course and everyone informed.

The outcome of the analysis stage of the decision-making process will itself create the need for an important decision. If on the basis of considered evidence the problem is important enough to be solved then the decision to proceed to the next stage of the process will be made. Some problems may not be regarded seriously enough to warrant full-scale treatment and can probably be dealt with by executive action. In this case the process will end at this stage.

3 Working out alternative solutions

Some problems seem to suggest obvious solutions. However, the temptation to go for the apparently obvious solution should be resisted as the modern proverb warns: 'Every complex problem has a simple solution, and it's wrong.' The fact is, of course, that the simple solution is sometimes the right one, but pursuing this as a general assumption can be dangerous.

During the process of preparing alternative solutions, deeper insights into the nature of the problem itself can often be gained, and

Stage 1 Identification

> What is the problem?
> How was it identified?
> What are the symptoms?

Stage 2 Discussion

> General discussion
> > (a) individuals
> > (b) agenda item at staff meeting

Stage 3 Examination

> Examination of the symptoms
> > Who will do it?
> > How will it be done?
> > How will it be recorded and presented (written or verbal)?
> > How long will it take?

Stage 4 Report

> Presentation of the report
> > Individual consideration
> > General discussion
> > Further consultation −governors
> >   −advisers
> >   −parents

Stage 5 Decision

> General discussion ⟶ Decision ⟨ No further action / Action ⟩
>
> Action ⟶ Work out alternative solutions

Figure 4.1 The analysis process

the risk of acting only for expediency reduced. Possible solutions need to be tested out against relevant criteria such as cost, time required, resources available, as well as the anticipated effect upon the various interest groups — children, teachers, non-teaching staff, parents etc. Essentially it is a process in which various solutions are related to differing costs and effects. Some solutions may be cheap in terms of financial outlay but prohibitive in terms of the time required for implementation; whereas others may involve too devastating an upheaval of the organization of the school.

Before a decision to adopt a particular solution can be made, the rationale of the competing alternatives must be presented for consideration. A checklist of relevant criteria should be prepared and applied to each alternative in turn.

Alternative solution checklist

PROBLEM:

SOLUTION No.:

COST
Initial
Renewal

RESOURCES
Books
Equipment
Stationery

CHANGES
Curriculum
design
Curriculum
content
Teaching
methods

TIME REQUIRED

Organization
Timetable
Staffing

EVALUATION
METHOD

EFFECT ON
Children
Teachers
Parents

This part of the decision-making process will involve a good deal of thinking on the part of those involved, and probably some meetings with individuals and groups.

A useful technique to try early on in this stage of the process is brainstorming. This involves a group meeting together to generate as many ideas as possible relevant to the solution of the problem under consideration. These should be noted down but not discussed, and there should be no criticism of any point raised or indeed any negative reaction at all. Wild ideas should be encouraged and nothing should be rejected because it sounds impractical. The emphasis should be on generating a quantity of ideas, a list of which should then be prepared and given to the group to discuss. At this stage some will be found to have real value, while others may have no relevance whatsoever. The virtue of the exercise is twofold. First, ideas can be generated in a climate where their justification is not an assumed precondition. It is surprising how reticent group members can be if they think they have to qualify every utterance they make. Second, the exercise provides excellent training in creative and imaginative problem-solving. Given the right conditions there are few who will fail to derive some satisfaction from it, and it is, incidentally, an excellent way of involving children in the decision-making process.

4 Choosing the best alternative

Now is the time to go for one particular solution. At this stage a decision is to be made affecting the future development of the school. The quality of the decision can only really be judged at some future time when its effects can be measured against its intentions. However there is more likelihood of success at this stage if all those participating in making the decision are adequately informed and given sufficient time for consideration and discussion.

The various alternative solutions should be presented as feasibility studies. Copies of the alternative solution checklist can be circulated some days before the general meeting to discuss them. Individual members of staff can seek further information, or points of clarification as necessary, from those involved in the generation of the various solutions.

The general meeting provides an opportunity for the competing schemes to be discussed. Each solution can be presented in turn and further points of information resolved. Some of the issues which need debating are contained in the following checklist:

1 *Resources*
   (a) Books   which books?
               how many?
               is immediate purchase necessary or can they be obtained over a number of years?

    (b) Equipment   which supplier?
                   how will it be allocated?
                   what about maintenance – wastage?
    (c) Stationery   any change from current position?

2 *Cost*
    (a) Capital outlay   this financial year?
                      future years?
    (b) Maintenance cost   future years? When will capital outlay be
                      required again?

3 *Changes*
    (a) Curriculum   how will the overall policy of the school be
                   affected?
                   what impact on transfer schools?
                   how will it affect continuity and progression?
                   will changes be introduced gradually a year at a
                   time?
    (b) Teaching   will staff need to change their methods?
                   do they have the skills they need?
                   what sort of INSET activities are necessary?

4 *Time*
    (a) how soon can implementation begin?
    (b) how soon before the new scheme is fully implemented?
    (c) will the new scheme take more time or less time than
        previously?

5 *Organization*
    (a) how will the new scheme affect specialist roles?
    (b) how will staff be deployed?
    (c) will usual timetable activities be affected?
    (d) how will shared resources be organized?

6 *Evaluation*
    (a) how will the scheme as a whole be monitored? who will do it?
    (b) how can the scheme be evaluated in relation to individual
        children?
    (c) when can results of evaluation be regarded as valid?
    (d) how will record-keeping and documentation be managed?

7 *Effects*
    (a) Children   what new opportunities does the scheme offer
                  in areas of motivation, interest, relevance, inte-
                  gration?
    (b) Teachers   what opportunities for developing new skills and
                  acquiring new qualities?
    (c) Parents   how will they be informed? will parents be involved?

A checklist such as this will go some way to ensure that all relevant
factors are taken into consideration in arriving at a decision. The
generation of the checklist is a vital part of the decision-making
process and needs its fair share of time and expertise.

Once the advantages and disadvantages of the various schemes have been considered it is time for the head to remind the meeting of any constraints bearing upon the decision. It is also wise to recap on the reasons for the present exercise and of the hopes and expectations for its outcomes. The way that the actual decision itself is made needs consideration. It is usually best to work by a process of elimination thereby giving the more worthy schemes adequate consideration. The head has a crucial role to play here and should move towards a decision by consensus, so that all members of staff can happily identify with the final outcome. If modifications or amendments to the scheme are necessary to gain this consensus the head will have to judge if these can be incorporated without devaluing the positive benefits of the preferred scheme.

5 Implementing the chosen solution

There is a tendency in some organizations to regard the decision-making process as complete once the decision about the best solution to the problem has been taken. There is a danger too that a new head might be tempted to move on to another area of problem-solving before the previous decisions have been fully implemented.

The implementation stage needs meticulous planning and an action programme which will initiate the necessary changes. The emphasis at this stage is on action rather than ideas and the implementation programme will need to take account of:

1 The tasks to be undertaken, arranged in order.
2 The dates by which each task needs to be completed.
3 The members of staff responsible for the tasks at each stage of development.
4 Procedures for dealing with the inevitable snags.

As the coordinator of this activity the head will need to be aware that the future success of the new scheme will to a great extent depend upon how smoothly the implementation operation proceeds. Physical help as well as advice will be needed.

6 Evaluating its effectiveness

Finally comes the assessment which will compare what happens with what should have happened, and this will be the subject of Chapter 9.

In Chapter 3 six functions of headship were identified. Fig. 4.2 (p. 52) emphasizes the iterative nature of these and relates them to the decision-making process. It combines the six functions with the six decision-making stages to produce thirty-six potential activities.

	Planning	Creating	Communicating	Motivating	Organizing	Controlling
Recognizing the problem						
Analysing the problem						
Working out alternative solutions						
Choosing the best solution						
Implementing the chosen solution						
Evaluating its effectiveness						

Figure 4.2   Decision-making tasks

This framework, like the managerial grid discussed earlier, is capable of expansion beyond the primary task of applying a function to a stage of decision-making to identify specific tasks. It needs to be stressed that the functions can occur in any order but the stages of the decision-making process are in a strict sequence. Fully completed the network would provide a comprehensive blueprint of the decision-making process and as such a clear and systematic guide.

The benefit of an exercise such as this is related to the amount of thought and imagination which is applied to it. It cannot be regarded as an insurance against poor decisions or faulty management.

Some heads may regard my perception of the decision-making process as far too simplistic to be helpful, while others will baulk at its constraining complexity. This particular model of decision-making is given as an example. What is important is that heads recognize that they will be judged by the results of what they do, and that it is necessary to give most serious consideration to the ways and means of achieving the results they intend, and to follow a clear and definite process.

Staff participation

Having described the process itself it is now necessary to consider the part played by individual teachers and the staff as a whole. Much will depend upon the head's inclination and capacity for sharing decision-making with colleagues. In this book the head will be regarded as a team leader.

Let us begin by examining some of the possible arrangements for decision-making in a primary school. A range of examples will be described ranging from the autocratic to the democratic.

```
    Autocratic              Democratic
      1     2     3     4     5     6
      |_____|_____|_____|_____|_____|
```

1 The head alone controls the decision-making process by making the decisions and then announcing them to the staff who are expected to comply.
2 The head still controls the process but having made a decision attempts to give reasons for it.
3 The head undertakes the early stages of the process then recommends to staff the preferred solution. Some modification to the proposals as a result of discussion will be allowed.
4 The head invites colleagues to share in the first three stages but then makes the final decision.

5   The head involves the staff at all stages but defines the criteria
    determining the choice of solution.
6   The head becomes an equal member of a corporate decision-
    making body.

During the past twenty years or so there has been a steady movement
away from the autocratic extreme, and in line with life generally there
is an increasing pressure to involve all levels of the work force in
decision-making. Some secondary schools are experimenting with a
democratic model which involves both staff and pupils, and these are
well documented. As yet there is little evidence to suggest that primary
schools are moving in the same direction, although the Free School
movement can be regarded as a most interesting departure from
tradition.

There are a number of reasons why a fully democratic model might
not work well in the somewhat intimate and informal atmosphere of
the primary school:

1   Since democratic decision-making operates on a majority choice
    basis there could be an inclination towards polarizing different
    viewpoints.
2   Majority choice becomes an alternative to creating a constructive
    consensus which attempts to reconcile conflicting needs and
    interests.
3   It would be necessary to redefine the authority and power structure
    within the school. There are far reaching implications for our
    education system in this, not least being the role of the head itself.
4   There would need to be an acceptance on the part of all concerned
    that collective responsibility and accountability go hand in hand
    with power sharing.
5   There is a danger that the decision-making structure would
    become an end in itself instead of the means to an end.
6   Under present primary school conditions there is not enough time
    available to make such a system workable.

Basically there are three main reasons why some form of participatory decision-making is desirable. First, teachers have considerable
autonomy in the classroom and the head has no choice but to delegate
teaching tasks to them. Because of the tenuous nature of the head's
power individual teachers can, and do, resist the pressure to follow the
head's policy for the school. The second reason is more positive and is
based on the principle that members of organizations more readily
support decisions they have had a share in making. Third, there is
likely to be an improvement in the quality of decisions made if all those
involved in the life of the school have the opportunity to participate in
solving problems relevant to them. If there is a genuine desire to share
power and also to accept the responsibility that goes with it, decision-

making can become a positive and dynamic force in the school, not only increasing the job satisfaction of all those involved, but helping to raise the level of identification of individual needs with those of the school as a whole.

Clearly some self examination by the head is necessary. The following questions may help to focus the main issues:

1 Do I as the head have the prerogative on decision-making?
2 Am I paid more than my colleagues to make the decisions, or to take responsibility for decisions made?
3 Is it desirable for the staff to take part in determining the way the school develops?
4 Are teachers, and non-teaching staff, able to undertake a decision-making role?
5 How much authority am I prepared to relinquish while at the same time continuing to accept responsibility for what is decided?

The answers to these questions, and the reasons for them, will say a great deal about an individual head's attitudes to headship in general, and about his or her own particular role expectations. Some heads for example may have an overwhelming desire to initiate a participatory structure, but given the conditions under which they work they can see no way that it could be achieved. Some heads have a great sense of personal identification with their schools and may feel that to relinquish power is to abrogate responsibility. It is a contentious issue but there are four further points worth making:

1 Even in quite autocratic régimes teachers are involved in decision-making to some extent.
2 There is an increasing demand for power sharing.
3 Most primary schools have some teachers on Scale 2, and some on Scale 3. It would seem natural that teachers who accept such appointments should be prepared to have an increased share in decision-making and to accept the responsibility that goes with it.
4 Any head who intends to introduce a system of participation in a school where none exists should think in terms of years rather than months for its successful innovation.

Good decision-making requires a lot of personal interaction. Some of this will take place between individuals on an informal basis, but much of it will need to be more formally structured. Staff meetings have not always been held in very high esteem by teachers, and this is understandable if they have been used by the head as a vehicle for issuing instructions or conveying information. In schools which employ participatory decision-making staff meetings are coming to be valued as a vital aspect of school organization.

One of the difficulties created by the staffing structure of primary schools it that there are virtually no opportunities for meetings during the normal course of a working day. The concept of the working lunch has come to be associated with a certain sacrificial romanticism in other organizations; in schools they are very often the only way that a staff can conduct its business. It is not surprising that 'out of school' meetings have become the subject of union politics, but a little sad, since a school will not derive much benefit from participatory decision-making if meetings are regarded as 'voluntary activities' or overtime.

There are a number of good reasons why formally constituted meetings should become a natural part of schools' decision-making processes. First, heads are able to demonstrate through their handling of meetings that they regard colleagues as partners in the decision-making enterprise, and not as instruments of a unilaterally formulated policy. Second, as staff become familiar with the process it is likely they will feel their status enhanced and respond with an increased determination to take a positive and dynamic part in it. Third, individual participants are much more likely to work actively to implement decisions they have given vocal support to.

Some consideration should be given to the size of decision-making groups — the ideal is between five and ten members. In meetings of this size there should be enough variety of interest, knowledge and experience to tackle problems imaginatively, and also sufficient opportunity for each member to become thoroughly involved in the discussion. Larger meetings have to be held, but smaller groups are much more effective in the early stages. If a decision requires the support of the whole staff it is useful to set up sub-groups which can submit reports, proposals or recommendations to the larger forum.

In a dynamic school, meetings become a natural part of the way of life. If a staff meeting is a rare event then it is unlikely to be part of a decision-making process. A head knows that when colleagues put in requests for meetings, or indeed set them up themselves, then participation is working.

Meetings should be purposeful and well conducted. Thought should be given to the physical setting in which meetings take place; the nature of the business to be discussed; the circulation of notes and agendas and the recording of the proceedings. Most meetings in primary schools take place in the staffroom. However informal the staff, it is important that a meeting is not casually slotted into a post-lunch marking session, or an after school cup of tea. Although many schools have no choice, it is worth considering holding formal meetings elsewhere. I once worked in a school where meetings were circulated round all the classrooms in turn, a strategy which had a number of beneficial side effects. The actual act of moving from a comfortable chair in the staffroom to sit around a table in another room can raise the sense of purpose and serve to focus individual minds on the business in hand.

Agendas are essential. No group can work efficiently within the limited time available in a primary school without knowing what the purpose of the meeting is. Some schools have a regular weekly meeting, and certainly most schools will create enough business to keep it fully employed. However meetings should never be held if there is no clear need for them. A distinction needs to be drawn between routine administrative meetings and those in which decisions about school policy, curriculum and organization are made. Administrative meetings are necessary and serve to reinforce communications, but wherever possible should be separated from the decision-making process.

Excessive formality is not in keeping with the spirit and ethos of most primary schools, but this should not inhibit a purposeful and business-like approach. Ideally, each member of staff should receive a copy of the agenda for a meeting a few days before it is held. This should contain the items to be discussed and also an indication if any important decisions are to be taken.

Sample agendas

Agenda for staff meeting about administrative matters

This copy for . . . .

Staff meeting to be held at 12.30, March 4th.

1 To fix dates for parents meetings
2 Report from Safety Representative
3 School trips and visits in summer term
4 Swimming Gala June 15th
5 End of term arrangements
6 AOB

Agenda for decision-making staff meeting

This copy for . . . .

Staff meeting to be held at 4.00, March 12th.

Purpose: To consider reports from sub-groups

1 Class allocations for next academic year.
2 Room allocations for next academic year.

Final decisions on these matters will be made at the meeting on March 19th.

An administrative meeting can usually deal with a fairly long agenda within the space of an hour, but decision-making meetings should have a short agenda so as to allow plenty of time for issues to be adequately discussed.

The question of chairmanship is also important. In some decision-making bodies the head always takes the chair, but in others the task is circulated between other members of staff. This is usually a matter the group itself can decide, but no one should be pressurized to accept the duty if they are reluctant. Much has been written about the art of chairmanship; perhaps the following list will serve to summarize the main points:

1   Aggression should be dealt with impartially. The chairman should restate the points made by the angry participant so that all are clear about what has been said. Anger should not be ignored, and objections should be fully explored.
2   Conflict is natural and indeed essential to good decision-making. It is wrong on the part of both heads and other members of staff to regard argument as implying disrespect. The chairman should use well-directed questions to get to the heart of the argument, and should not allow disputes over generalizations.
3   Silences can be embarrassing. The chairman should have the courage to sit them out.
4   The chairman should not:
    (a) inhibit free discussion
    (b) allow red herrings
    (c) overwork the meeting.
5   The chairman should:
    (a) specify the purpose of the meeting at the beginning and at intervals as necessary.
    (b) summarize main ideas and underline the progress of the meeting.
    (c) keep the discussion moving forward by questioning individuals, and encouraging them to speak from their specialist knowledge and experience.

An important aspect of the head's leadership function in dealing with decision-making is to know when to work through the staff, and when through individuals or small groups. Flexibility is the best plan and it is unwise to make the process too highly structured. Above all the head needs to be clear about the purposes of the meetings and to communicate these to all who take part. Careful planning and good chairmanship can avoid the need for too many meetings by getting more out of the ones that are held.

The question of attendance at staff meetings is sometimes raised. If staff meetings really are occasions when important decisions are made in a democratic way then staff will not want to miss them. Regarding them as compulsory does nothing to assist the development of trusting relationships which are so essential to a healthy school. There will be occasions when individuals will be unable to attend but much tension can be avoided by calling meetings well in advance — even setting the dates a term ahead if necessary — and not calling too many meetings at very short notice. When team work is really succeeding members will be anxious to attend. When they cannot, it is to the team as a whole they send their apologies for absence.

References

DES (1978) *Primary Education in England: A Survey by HM Inspectors of Schools* London: HMSO

HOLT, J. (1973) *Freedom and Beyond* Harmondsworth: Penguin

5 Planning the Curriculum

There are a number of similarities between the role-defining exercise outlined in Chapter 1 and that of planning the curriculum. For a start, the same four categories can be used to analyse the constraints and influences on the curriculum:

1 prescriptions
2 expectations
3 situations
4 predilections.

1 Prescriptions

Like the British constitution, our educational curriculum defies precise definition. Yet all those who have been through the education system have a view about what it is, and how it should be organized.

The Education Act 1944 is very coy on the subject of the curriculum. There are few places where the word 'curriculum' occurs; in other places there is mention of 'secular instruction', but virtually nothing about what the children in schools should actually be doing. The well known exception is section 25 paragraphs (1) and (2):

25 (1) Subject to the provisions of this section, the school day in every county school . . . shall begin with collective worship on the part of all pupils in attendance at the school. . . .

(2) Subject to the provisions of this section, religious instruction shall be given in every county school. . . .

However, further clues are provided in Section 23 (1) which states:

'The secular instruction to be given to pupils, save in so far as may be otherwise provided by the rules of government, be under the control of the local education authority.' The implication of that firm and unequivocal statement is that central government has nothing to do with determining the curriculum. So what have the local authorities done? In most cases they have delegated the task to the governing bodies of schools. The model Rules of Government have been referred to earlier, and it will be recalled that they place responsibility for the conduct of the curriculum with the governors.

In some local authorities, particularly those which operate a local inspectorate, rather than an advisory service, prescriptions might be said to exist in the recommendations put forward during school visits, or following formal inspections. Also those authorities which continue to select at age 11+ are in some measure attempting to determine the nature of the curriculum that exists in their primary schools.

2 Expectations

What was found lacking by way of prescription is more than compensated for here. It is a tribute to our national system that curriculum prescriptions have not been found necessary, despite the clamour for them from some directions. Flexibility and adaptability are maintained by virtue of the fact that prescriptive constraints do not inhibit schools from responding to change, as and when they feel it necessary. The reason that our primary schools have attracted the interest and admiration of so many other countries is that they have been encouraged to develop new curriculum programmes, more flexible school designs and more informal teaching methods. It is encouraging too, that while standards of performance have been maintained, the quality of life and the range of experiences for children in our primary schools have increased enormously.

So what are the spheres of influence that converge upon a school and help to determine the curriculum that it operates? They exist as a set of expectations which derive from:

1 curriculum traditions
2 children
3 teachers
4 governors
5 parents
6 informed opinion
7 public debate.

The traditional assumptions about what a primary school curriculum should be are slow to change, and even so called 'progressive' institutions offer a range of courses that would compare closely with models stretching back before compulsory schooling was introduced in 1870.

Teachers get set in their ways too, and are likely to develop their curriculum philosophy early in their careers. A first appointment can often be very influential in establishing a teacher's value position, and can set a pattern of assumptions that does not always respond readily to change in later years.

During the 1960s and early 1970s many primary schools experienced something of a crisis in parental confidence. The changeover to a more integrated and flexible curriculum, and the adoption of 'discovery' and child-centred education, left many parents perplexed about what their children were doing in their primary school classrooms. The fact was, that for the first time in the history of education, the pattern of schooling undertaken by the children of the time was in many cases very different from that which their parents had experienced. The generation gap phenomenon of 'what was good enough for me is good enough for you', together with a genuine confusion about the 'new maths' particularly, meant that schools acquired a new function — that of explaining the curriculum to a bemused body of parents. Today, of course, parents play a much more active part in the life of schools, a move which has been strengthened by their presence on governing bodies in many local authorities. Most primary schools today, conscious of the value of a supportive parent body, go to some pains to explain and demonstrate the work they are doing. Few curriculum decisions can afford to disregard the views and attitudes of parents.

Despite a clearly defined authority over the curriculum, governing bodies have demonstrated a reluctance to become involved in the details of curriculum planning. However, the Taylor Committee in their report *A New Partnership for Our Schools* (DES 1977a) was determined to see this authority more precisely defined, as the following summary recommendations show:

37 The governing body should be given by the local authority the responsibilty for setting the aims of the school, for considering the means by which they are pursued, for keeping under review the school's progress towards them, and for deciding upon action to facilitate such progress.

39 The governing body should invite the headteacher in consultation with his staff to prepare papers setting out the means by which they propose to pursue the aims adopted.

34 Information and advice on the life and activities of the school should be brought together in each school with the purpose of creating an effective but unobtrusive information system for the governing body. The headteacher should be made responsible for the development of the system, working with general guidance provided by the governing body about the aspects of the school's activities on which information is required and the form in which it is required.

46 Every governing body should produce a first general appraisal of the school's progress, however incomplete, within four years of its formation.

The exact term for subsequent appraisal should be decided by the local education authority after consultation with the governing bodies of the schools in its area.

If such proposals as these do eventually become part of educational law, then a governing body will form an important part of the school's decision-making process, and curriculum planning will have an altogether different complexion.

Local authority influence on the curriculum has already been mentioned. In some authorities advisers, in addition to the purely advisory work, fulfil an executive function and are involved in appointments and promotions procedures. In these circumstances their power to influence curriculum development is likely to be greater. The content of the programme of in-service courses for teachers can also provide some clues to an authority's curriculum expectations. But perhaps the strongest influence a local authority wields is almost inevitably a financial one. In order to promote certain curriculum schemes some authorities are prepared to make extra allocations of money available. Even so, local authority influence over the curriculum continues to be fairly minimal, and few heads would regard their LEA as the chief of those to be satisfied.

Schools do respond positively to informed opinion. During the last ten years curriculum planning has continued to have regard for the Plowden Report (DES 1967), and more particularly for the full and detailed report of the Bullock Committee *A Language for Life* (DES 1975). Also much discussion and re-examination of assumptions have been stimulated by the various Black Papers (Cox and Dyson 1969a and b), but more particularly by the research findings of Neville Bennett in his *Teaching Styles and Pupil Progress* (Bennet 1976). The Government Green Paper *Education in Schools* (DES 1977b) with its talk of a core curriculum has succeeded in bringing about curriculum evaluation at both local and national level. More recently, publication of the HMI survey (DES 1978) has provided a more fundamental insight into the state of primary education than had hitherto been attempted, and this document is likely to be the stimulus for curriculum development for the next decade.

Public opinion is to some extent informed by the professional dialectic of teaching, but politicians, employers, economists, academics and church leaders also have their disparate opinions to add. In times of economic stress, education becomes something of a social scapegoat. As we move inexorably towards greater structural unemployment, the question of how we should be educating our children for a future which will be very different from the present, is bound to occupy those whose responsibility it is to decide the nature of the curriculum.

Having considered a range of expectations of which most schools

would be aware, we now come to those factors which are specific to
individual schools.

3 Situations

The following list cannot be comprehensive, but serves to identify the
sorts of internal influences which can affect the content and design of
an individual school's curriculum:

1   design of the building
2   history and traditions
3   finance
4   resources
5   curriculum as it exists
6   decision-making process
7   school organization
8   transfer and admission arrangements
9   catchment area
10 attitudes.

The list needs little elaboration except perhaps for the last item. There
has been a tendency to give little attention to the influence of human
factors on the way a school develops. Chapter 3 stressed how important
it was for the head to try and understand the human climate of the
school and to have regard for the nature and quality of personal and
group interaction. Good teachers make good schools, and the most
telling measure of the quality of the curriculum in a school is the
extent to which the achievements of the children measure up to
expectation.

4 Predilections

The final set of considerations derive from the hopes and aspirations
of those whose task it is to implement the curriculum, namely the head
and the staff. Since most teaching in primary schools is based on
general practice, rather than specialism, primary teachers are
involved in the whole curriculum. Primary heads when first
appointed, and with some years of general practice behind them, tend
to have a somewhat idealistic view of the curriculum, and it comes as
something of a shock to find that changing the way the school goes
about its business is not simply a matter of rationalizing a vision. For
the head the task of curriculum planning is essentially one of relating
what is theoretically desirable to what is practically possible.

The need for the head to have a clearly formulated philosophy of
education has been stressed earlier in the book. Certainly in terms
of leadership capability, heads are expected to be initiators and

innovators, and to have formulated for themselves answers to current questions on curriculum and organization. Teachers gain security and comfort from the knowledge that their head is not only a good organizer and competent administrator, but also a deep thinker who is well able to relate general theory to the specific school situation. Heads should not diminish their visions, even if the forces opposing realization seem overwhelming, nor should they be tempted to set inferior goals for themselves. The challenge of headship is to bring a vision to reality, and the trials and tribulations of achieving that is what headship is all about. It is certainly not a job for the faint-hearted.

In practical terms, the head's task in planning and developing the curriculum of the school is to create an organizational climate which is conducive to self examination, secure in its capacity to solve problems collectively, and above all flexible. Given the fact that teachers exercise considerable autonomy in the classroom, the only successful approach to curriculum planning is a cooperative one, in which all teachers are members of a decision-making team and play a full and active part.

The exercise of planning the curriculum has three distinct stages:

1   establishing goals
2   determining methods
3   evaluating results.

The aim of the exercise is to define what children shall learn, how they will learn it, and how well they have succeeded in doing so.

Establishing goals

From the amount of attention that this area of education now receives it could be thought that 'aims and objectives' was a new invention. What is even more apparent is a confusion over terms. Definitions in education tend to beg as many questions as they answer, but since my purpose is a practical rather than a semantic one, I offer the following:

Curriculum: a school's intentions for its learners.
Goals: general statements about what the school wishes to achieve.
Aims: specific statements of intention, formulated in terms of the desirable condition of a child's education after the completion of a curriculum programme.
Objectives: short-term tactical targets, which derive from the aims and indicate the stages of progress towards their achievement.

The relationship between these elements can be conceived as:

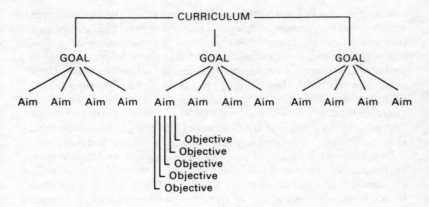

Portraying the elements in a hierarchy seems to place too much emphasis on the philosophy and not enough on the smaller components which constitute the daily activities in most schools. The following diagram, employing the same components, changes the perspective and puts the whole curriculum in the heart of the school rather than at its edge.

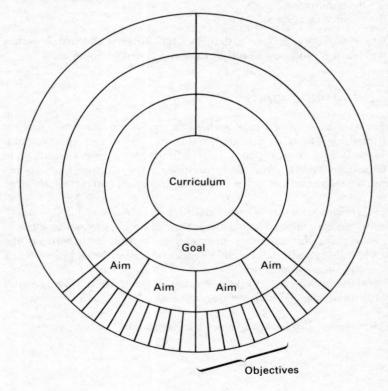

What is important is that the relationship between the parts and the whole is easily understood, for unless individual teachers recognize that even the simplest objective has a vital link with the overall philosophy, the school will run the risk of paying only lip-service to its declared intentions. It is important too, to remember that aims and objectives are the intended outcomes of activities, they are not the activities themselves. The nature and extent of the intentions are, of course, a matter of choice and judgment for individual schools. The essential point about their description is that everyone involved shall know what they mean.

Curriculum design is a well-documented area of research and opinion and it is not the intention of this book to enter the debate about which particular approach is to be preferred — that is an issue for each school to decide. What is important is that some consideration is given to the particular approach to be adopted. By way of illustration two basic models will be examined; a subject-based approach; and a personal-growth model.

During the past three years many heads will have been involved in the exercise of comparing their own schools with the findings of the HMI survey of primary education (DES 1978). Annex B of this document is a summary of the schedules which HMI used in their inspection of the survey classes. For our purposes it is the particular way the curriculum has been analysed that is of interest. Their framework is as follows:

1 Aesthetic and physical education
   (i)   Art and crafts
   (ii) Music
   (iii) Physical education
2 Language and literacy
   (i)   Reading
   (ii) Writing
3 Mathematics
4 Science
5 Social abilities
   (i)   Social, moral and religious education
   (ii) Geography and history

In addition to these there is a schedule which outlines aspects of organization and methods of working likely to affect the implementation of the curriculum.

With this basic analysis it is possible to expand these categories according to the framework illustrated earlier. Before considering this process in more detail let us look at the second example, the personal growth model. This is contained in the teachers' guide to the Schools Council Aims in Primary Education Project, *Aims into Practice in the Primary School* (Ashton, Kneen and Davies 1975).

The following technique for identifying aims was developed in cooperation
with very many teachers in the course of the Aims of Primary Education
Project. It consists of a simple convenient device for reminding teachers of
the possible areas in which they are likely to think that aims are appropriate.
It can be represented diagrammatically.

Related to:	Aims to do with		
	Knowledge	Skills	Qualities
Intellectual development	8	13	2
Physical development	2	4	1
Aesthetic development	0	4	4
Spiritual/religious development	2	0	3
Emotional/personal development	2	2	10
Social/moral development	1	6	8

Figure 5.1   Personal growth model for identifying aims

The numbers show how the 72 aims defined were distributed. As an
insight into the process of curriculum planning this book is strongly
recommended.

These two examples provide us with different approaches to the
basic approach to curriculum design. There are many other
approaches too, and in practice it is likely that any particular curriculum design will have regard to both the subject classification of the
HMI survey and the personal growth aspect of the Schools Council
Project.

So far we have established a basic framework for the curriculum
plan. We can get nearer to the finished article by defining the
practical steps that need to be taken.

1 *Establish framework*: e.g. subject or personal growth model.
2 *Define goals*: a list of general agreed statements linked to each
element of the framework.
3 *Generate aims*: a checklist of items related to each goal and
making reference to what the child is expected to learn.
4 *Specify objectives*: breaking down each of the aims into precise
statements of intent. They should specify the type of learning that is
intended, e.g. knowledge, skill or quality.

To see how this can work out in practice let us take the example of a
multicultural primary school which is anxious to create a curriculum
which has due regard for the very different backgrounds from which
the children come. During their final two years in the junior department the children take part in a world studies course[1] which forms part
of the social studies programme. The section of the curriculum plan
relating to this particular course is as follows:

GOAL
Through a programme of social studies to develop:
 (i)   moral − ethical values
 (ii) religious ideas and values
 (iii) geographical awareness
 (iv) historical awareness

AIMS
Related to the course in world studies (the other courses forming part
of the social studies programme were
 (i) religious studies
(ii) community studies)
1 Knowledge
      (i) of one's own society and culture
      (ii) of other societies and cultures
2 Attitudes
      (i)   to develop a positive self image
      (ii) to encourage curiosity
      (iii) to develop open-mindedness
      (iv) to appreciate other cultures
      (v)   to develop justice and fairness
3 Skills of
      (i)   inquiry
      (ii) expression
      (iii) empathy

---

[1]The aims and objectives for the World Studies course are based on work done by Robin
Richardson, Adviser for Multicultural Education, Berkshire. The complete checklist is
contained in: Fisher, S. *et al.* (1980) *Ideas into Action − Curriculum for a Changing
World: A Handbook for Teachers written by Teachers* London: World Studies Project

OBJECTIVES

Related to the knowledge aims:

1(i)   Knowledge of one's own society and culture

    1(i)a Pupils should be able to *describe* the culture and society to which they themselves belong, and their own place in this wider context.

    1(i)b Pupils should be able to *explain* how their society works, and why aspects of their own society and culture are as they are.

    1(i)c Pupils should be able to make *judgments* about what is valuable and harmful in their own society and culture, both from their own point of view and that of others.

1(ii) Knowledge of other societies and cultures.

    1(ii)a Pupils should be able to *describe* the main feature of certain societies and cultures other than their own, including minority cultures within their own society.

    1(ii)b Pupils should be able to *explain* the background of certain other societies and cultures, and how their members perceive themselves and the world.

    1(ii)c Pupils should be able to *make judgments* about other societies and cultures.

Similar sets of statements for every area of the curriculum have a number of distinct purposes:

1   They indicate to pupils what is expected of them. This is a very under-used strategy in the primary school and one that can helpfully be employed right from infant stage.

2   They provide information for: the head and staff; the governors; the LEA; prospective parents.

3   They encourage teachers to be aware of and explicit about their intentions.

4   They help teachers working at different stages to see how the separate parts relate to an overall plan.

5   They help teachers to decide for, or against, specific methods and approaches.

6   They help teachers to reflect, both individually and collectively, how well a programme of work is developing.

7   They provide guidelines and checklists for the evaluation and assessment of what pupils have learnt.

From the practical point of view one of the key questions facing the head is how to achieve agreement on such a fundamental issue as what the curriculum should contain. If planning is undertaken systematically, stage by stage, then the exercise is more likely to be successful. The stages need to be related to a time sequence so that all those involved know what is being aimed at, and when it should be achieved.

For agreement on a whole curriculum at least a year will be necessary if attention is to be given to the finer details as well as the broad issues. Revisions or reviews of a particular curriculum area will need at least a term.

Curriculum planning schedule

Stage	Activities	Resulting action	Completion date
1 Rationale	Consideration and discussion of reasons, purposes and outcomes of the exercise.	Circulate document: 'Summary of Considerations'	Autumn h/t
2 Framework	(i) Consideration of alternative frameworks (ii) Choice of framework	Circulate alternative frameworks	End of Nov.
3 Goals	(i) Brainstorm goals (ii) Choice of goals	Circulate long list of goals Circulate selected list	Beginning of Spring term
4 Aims	(i) Brainstorm aims in each category (ii) Select aims for each category	Circulate long lists Circulate selected lists	Spring h/t
5 Objectives	(i) Brainstorm objectives (ii) Select objectives	Circulate long lists Circulate selected lists	Beginning of Summer term
6 Design of document	(i) Prepare draft designs (ii) Select design	Circulate draft designs	End April
7 Final revisions	Editing and checking of agreed lists	Circulation of proof copy	Summer h/t
8 Final draft	Typing and duplication of document		Beginning of Autumn term
9 Circulation	Circulation of copies	Presentation at governors meeting	

A planning schedule such as the one on page 71 will serve to outline the main tasks ahead and provide an indication of the time available for preparations and discussions.

An important consideration is who is to be involved in the planning exercise. If whole-staff agreement is to be achieved all members of staff have a part to play, but in reality it is unnecessary and inefficient to involve everyone at all stages. In secondary schools detailed curriculum decisions are made within departments. In the primary school most teachers are involved in the whole curriculum and the departmental structure tends to be by stages of development rather than by subjects. In terms of planning the curriculum for the primary age-range staff can be grouped into three stages — infant, lower junior and upper junior. What needs to be determined is which elements of the curriculum plan require whole-staff involvement and which can be delegated to individuals or small groups. In very small schools, where teaching in classes of mixed age-groups has always been the tradition, it is likely that all staff will be involved at all stages. In larger schools it is possible to divide up the detailed work once agreement on the overall curriculum goals has been reached. Certainly in the early stages of planning a wide measure of association with decisions is essential. In the interests of continuity and progression from one stage to another it is important that the decisions of sub-groups are submitted for full staff consideration and approval.

The particular problems of curriculum planning in small schools is referred to in the HMI survey (DES 1978).

8.53 In small schools the numbers of teachers on the staff is likely to be too small to provide the necessary specialist knowledge in all parts of the curriculum. The teachers in a group of schools can profitably share their skills in planning programmes of work and a number of small schools (and large) have benefited from doing so as a result of their own enterprise, under the guidance of local authority advisers, through teachers' centres or with the help of Schools Council and other curricular projects.

The head's leadership qualities are the key factor in bringing this planning exercise to a satisfactory conclusion. Part of the training for headship should include information about and practice in the techniques of corporate decision-making. While a considerable amount of work is being undertaken in university departments of education on the process of cooperative decision-making, little has yet been done to identify and disseminate those techniques and activities likely to be helpful to groups such as the staff of a primary school. One particularly rich source of ideas for participatory decision-making is *Debate and Decision* (Richardson, Flood and Fisher 1979). This booklet sets out to explore the ways a staff of a comprehensive school could go about developing the curriculum. Although it is related to the field of multicultural education and secondary pupils, the book does set out a series of in-service activities which can easily be adapted for use in the primary staffroom.

In the process of establishing goals for the curriculum it is important to remember that the document that results is not a teaching scheme, and the aims and objectives are not necessarily arranged in the same order as they would be taught. So having decided what learning opportunities the school intends for its pupils, the question of implementation arises.

Determining methods

There are basically three questions to be answered now that the curriculum has been established:

1   who will teach what?
2   how will it be taught?
3   when will it be taught?

The way these questions are answered will to a great extent depend upon the range of teaching styles represented on the staff, and this is an issue which requires some consideration. A key problem for the head is whether to aim for uniformity of practice, or to accept that teaching style is a matter for individuals to decide for themselves. Pursued for its own sake, uniformity of practice could lead to a dull school, while a certain variety of approach would seem to make for a more dynamic one. The way teachers operate within the classroom perhaps receives less consideration than the content of the curriculum itself.[1] A wise and well integrated staff will wish to impose upon themselves certain conditions in relation to their particular teaching methods if they are to be successful in achieving their corporate intentions. That there is a need for agreement on this issue is illustrated by the diagram on page 74 which shows the variety of journeys a single child could follow during his or her four years in a two-form entry junior school.

The illustration ignores the vertical-grouping pattern that many primary schools adopt. Although it is unlikely, it is possible that a child entering class 1a in a particular year could follow any of the various paths to arrive in either 4a or 4b some years later. This raises an important question. Should there be an assumption that, implicit

[1] 1980 has seen the publication of the reports of the ORACLE project based at Leicester University School of Education. The reports provide important insights into teaching style and their effect on pupil performance. Galton, M. *et al.* (1980) *Inside the Primary Classroom* London: Routledge & Kegan Paul; Galton, M. and Simon, B. (eds) (1980) *Progress and Performance in the Primary Classroom* London: Routledge & Kegan Paul.

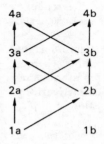

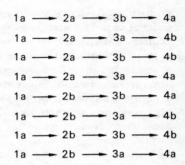

in the design of the curriculum and particularly in the determination of teaching methods to be employed, the curriculum goals laid down will not be adversely affected by the nature of the journey that a child follows through the school? In other words, will the child get the same deal whichever journey is undertaken? One of the essential qualities of primary schooling is the particular relationships that a teacher establishes with individual children and with the class as a whole. However, in terms of the teaching styles preferred by individual members of staff, there should be an agreement that teaching style itself will not prejudice progress towards the agreed educational goals of the school.

One of the main objectives of the taking stock exercise discussed in Chapter 2 is the analysis of the teaching styles employed. One of the interesting by-products of Bennett's *Teaching Style and Pupil Progress* (Bennett 1976) was his identification and description of a range of twelve teaching styles. I am surprised that this important typology has not received more attention (see footnote p. 73). One of the important purposes of the taking stock exercise is to attempt to determine to what extent the range of teaching styles represented in a school does appear to inhibit progress towards the realization of aims. There is a delicate balance between prescription and autonomy in this matter, and the head should be concerned to initiate open discussion which will allow all aspects of the question to be examined. It sometimes needs stressing that teaching methods are only the means by which agreed aims are pursued, they are not ends in themselves. Not until it becomes second nature for teachers to talk openly with each other about the way they work, and to accept that their own approach is only as good as they themselves make it, will the climate be conducive to group agreement on teaching methods.

Before discussion can be worthwhile, each member of staff should be in a position to:

1   understand the nature of the learning process across the age range represented by the school;

2   be familiar with the teaching methods employed in the preceeding
    year, and the year following. For a first-year junior teacher this will
    involve liaison with the final-year infant teacher, and for the
    fourth-year junior teacher links with the secondary school;
3   understand and appreciate the particular teaching methods
    employed by all colleagues in the school;
4   understand, and be able to describe and explain, how they them-
    selves approach and perform their teaching tasks.

The main purpose of seeking agreement about teaching methods is
to ensure that the children's educational achievements are not
inhibited because individual teachers work in different ways. In the
example illustrated, the teacher receiving children from both 2a and
2b should be able to proceed with the new year's work on the basis of
certain assumptions. However, difficulties can sometimes arise as the
following example demonstrates.

At the beginning of the new academic year the teacher of 2a found:
1   The children from 1a had been taught subtraction by decomposition, those from 1b by equal addition. Should he: (a) continue
both methods; (b) teach the 1a children equal addition; (c) teach
the 1b children decomposition?
2   The children from 1a were used to doing rough copies of their
written work which was then copied up. The 1b children always
worked straight into their exercise books.
3   The children from 1a had been taught an italic script in pen,
those from 1b were still printing in pencil.

This example raises a most important consideration — that of continuity and progression from one phase of education to another, and
within each phase from one year to another. One distinct advantage of
vertical-grouping is that it helps to avoid the disruption to learning
that can occur when children move on to a new teacher each year. In
these situations far too much time is wasted at the beginning of each
academic year in attempting to discover the stage each child has
reached in the various curriculum areas and in striving to establish a
different set of learning habits.
   While it is right and proper that teachers should work in their
preferred way, it is vital that time is afforded for discussion and consideration of the general issues of continuity and progression, and
more specifically that the sorts of problems illustrated in the example
are identified and dealt with through the decision-making procedure.

Documenting the curriculum

Some schools seem to achieve miraculous results without having any written documents about the curriculum. There will always be those who operate according to some form of divine inspiration, and they will have no need of a book like this anyway, but documenting the major principles and practices of a school is important for a number of reasons:

1   It shows that the school curriculum is not the product of whim or fancy, but the result of thought and deliberation.
2   It provides a source of information and reference for the staff, the governors, the parents and the local authority.
3   It facilitates accountability. Each of the governors can have a personal copy of curriculum documents which will both inform and also invite a more active participation in the work of the school.
4   It aids development. Future decisions are the result of earlier ones and curriculum documents provide evidence of these.
5   It facilitates the induction of new teachers. There can be no virtue in a system which places the new teacher in a position of having to find out what the curriculum is.
6   It is good management to record the important decisions that an organization makes about itself and the way it should work.

What then are the best ways of recording a school's curriculum intentions?

The school handbook

Earlier it was suggested that the school curriculum could be visualized in diagrammatic form, and while such a diagram is useful in helping to relate the parts to the whole in terms of agreed goals and their attendant aims and objectives, a set of statements is a more complete format for such an important declaration of intent. It is becoming fashionable for schools to issue handbooks to parents and these can be a most useful instrument for conveying school philosophy.[1] The vast majority of parents are interested and concerned in the way that the school sets about its work and one of the responsibilities that most heads acknowledge is that of keeping parents informed of school policy. A booklet which states briefly the philosophy upon which the school organization is based, with details and information about the curriculum, its aims, content and method, can provide an important link between teachers and parents. It will contain matters that will generate discussion, and perhaps some argument, but will stand as evidence of what the school believes in, and what it intends to achieve. Certainly no school should find it necessary to conceal its policy.

[1] The 1981 Education Act now requires schools to issue a handbook to prospective parents.

The staff handbook

A school booklet will not carry the finer detail of the curriculum which teachers will need. A staff handbook, or folder, containing a complete set of statements about the school's curriculum aims and objectives can provide a source of reference for all teachers, and particularly those who have only recently joined the staff. Schools will vary in their approach here, and while some will be content with general guidelines of work to be covered, others will need more detailed documentation in the form of syllabuses, programmes of work, schemes and checklists.

Since a school curriculum tends to undergo a process of gradual change, curriculum documentation should not be allowed to create a sense of immutability. One of the dangers of commiting a curriculum to paper is the sense of finality associated with the printed word. Staff members will need reminding that what curriculum papers state are certain agreements made by a school staff at a particular stage in its development. To give some emphasis to this point it is useful to date the document clearly, and perhaps to append the names of those involved in the decision-making process at that time. Every effort should be made to keep the documentation abreast of developments through supplements, additions, deletions and where necessary, complete revisions.

Statements about the organization structure will indicate the role each member of the teaching team will play. These will be concerned with both class and special responsibilities. The next chapter will deal with this in some detail.

A major factor to be considered is time, both in terms of a working week and an academic year. While a number of heads ask teachers to submit weekly or even termly forecasts of their teaching programme, fewer perhaps see a year plan as the essential core of the year to be covered. The two can be distinguished as follows:

Year plan: an outline of the curriculum programme for the academic year, related to the aims of the curriculum.
Term plan: a more detailed specification of particular subject programmes, related to the objectives of the curriculum.

The one document with which all teachers are familiar is the timetable. While this has little relationship with its secondary school counterpart, it does serve the useful purpose of designating the occupation of shared areas such as the hall, the library and the television room.

Evaluating results

Central to the planning of any major organizational activity should be determining how the success of that activity is to be measured. Successful planning leads to a close relationship between intentions and outcomes, and the purpose of evaluation is to assess the nature of that relationship. A school curriculum is a device to bring about certain fundamental changes in the abilities, attitudes and aspirations of children. If it suceeds it is because it has done what it was intended to do. If it fails it does so because the intentions were misguided, or the methods employed were faulty. Evaluation is necessary if such defects are to be corrected.

A curriculum plan cannot be considered complete until decisions have been made about how its effectiveness will be measured. A school's record-keeping system is essentially a device to monitor the curriculum, although frequently it is regarded as a means of ensuring children's progress. The business of evaluation may seem somewhat remote when a future project is being discussed but it is essential that the planning process gives adequate attention to each of the three constituent elements – goals, methods and evaluation. Each element is concerned with a vital question:

1 What are we intending to achieve?
2 By what means can we realize our intentions?
3 How will we know if we have succeeded?

So that while the planning process is about making decisions about a more desirable future, it needs to incorporate machinery for assessing if the outcomes were the intended ones.

The school record-keeping system is essentially the documentary aspect of evaluation. Much has been written on the subject, and at the time of writing the results of a Schools Council project are awaited with much interest.[1]

Only a head appointed to a new school will be faced with the exciting but awesome task of planning and implementing a new curriculum. Most heads inherit a curriculum and have to make of it what they can. Whichever is the case the time will come when aspects of the curriculum will need to be examined with a view to changes being made. In order to keep change and innovation to manageable proportions, curriculum development should be regarded as a long-term issue. Major curriculum revisions can take anything up to a year to plan and anything over a year to implement. For this reason some device is necessary to maintain this sense of proportion. An annual curriculum review can fulfil this purpose. In a sense it is a process rather than an event, involving as it does the various threads of experience over one year to inform the plans for the next. The review should be built in to the decision-making structure of the school, and provide

[1]Clift, P., Weiner, G. and Wilson, E. (1981) *Record Keeping in Primary Schools* London: Macmillan Educational.

the means by which teachers can relate current experience to recent developments and future needs.

The key features of a curriculum review are:

1   an annual report
2   discussion and consideration of the report
3   formulation of recommendations
4   action programme
5   necessary amendments to curriculum documentation.

The report itself will consist mainly of the proceedings of curriculum meetings held during the preceding year. These will have been concerned with problems that have arisen and for which solutions have been found. In summarizing the curriculum developments during the year the report should attempt to describe the results of changes implemented during the year, problems arising in other curriculum areas and possible areas of development. Such a report presents the opportunity to take stock, to assess progress and to identify new needs. It allows the teaching team the chance to evaluate the effectiveness of its decisions in the light of experience.

From time to time the head has to account to the governing body for the work of the school. This usually takes the form of a report which is included as an agenda item at the termly meeting of governors, and can often generate the main discussion. One copy of the report will be retained by the local authority and form part of the official records of the school. It is through this report that the head is presented with an excellent opportunity to involve the governors in the running of the school and to invite their participation. The very least that a head should do is to make sure that the governors are well informed about the curriculum and are consulted when major innovation is under consideration. This may involve a departure from traditional practice, and the forging of a more dynamic relationship between the teaching staff of the school and its governing body.

The report to the governors is the formal means by which the head discharges accountability. In some local authorities there are specially printed forms which the head is expected to fill in, which are read out at the governors' meeting by the clerk. Apart from the limitations imposed by forms this is an inefficient way of dealing with such an important aspect of the head's work. It is much better for the head to design and compose a report, have it duplicated and send a copy to each member of the governing body a week or two before the meeting. While the report should deal with what has happened in the school since the last report, it should also refer to the future. Papers summarizing plans for curriculum change and development can be attached to the report and these will help to prepare the governors for subsequent discussion. Ideally curriculum papers should be prepared by the teacher who has responsibility for that area of the curriculum. That member of staff can also be invited to be present at the meeting when the item is dealt with. Another possibility is for the governors to appoint a curriculum sub-committee which can liaise with the teachers concerned and then report back to the full meeting.

The subject of the head's report receives a chapter to itself in *The School Governors' and Managers' Handbook and Training Guide*. (Burgess and Sofer 1978) The chapter begins as follows:

> The head's report to the governors should be the real matter of the meeting; it is the formal occasion at which the head gives an account of his stewardship and the governors fulfil their duty of overseeing the conduct and curriculum of the school. However actual experience does not always match this theoretical picture. It is not an uncommon complaint that the head's report, often occuring at the end of the agenda, can be delivered and listened to somewhat perfunctorily, and appears to be no more than a catalogue of visitors and visits, and successes in the swimming gala and daffodil-growing competition.

The head can do much to overcome this unhappy reputation.

Many governors are uncertain of their precise role in the decision-making structure of the school. They will certainly not feel involved if they are not consulted and not invited into school to see for themselves what is going on. The head can do much to increase a sense of involvement. Few governors will refuse a personal invitation to come to the school for a specific purpose and once they know their presence is welcomed and their advice valued they will be less reluctant to visit. A governing body fully involved in the work of the school is not only highly desirable in management terms, but when it begins to feel an essential part of the educational enterprise it can help and support the school.

References

ASHTON, P., KNEEN, P., DAVIES, F. (1975) *Aims into Practice in the Primary School* London: Hodder and Stoughton.

BENNETT, N. (1976) *Teaching Styles and Pupil Progress* London: Open Books

BURGESS, T. and SOFER, A.(1978) *The School Governors' and Managers' Handbook* London: Kogan Page

COX, C.B. and DYSON, A.F. (eds) (1969) *Fight for Education: A Black Paper* Critical Quarterly Society

COX, C.B. and DYSON, A.E. (eds) (1969) *Black Paper Two: The Crisis in Education* Critical Quarterly Society

DES (1967) *Children and Their Primary Schools* (The Plowden Report) London: HMSO

DES (1975) *A Language for Life* (The Bullock Report) London: HMSO

DES (1977a) *A New Partnership for Our Schools* (The Taylor Report) London: HMSO

DES (1977b) *Education in Schools:A Consultative Document* Cmnd 6869 London: HMSO

DES (1978) *Primary Education in England* London: HMSO

RICHARDSON, R., FLOOD, M., FISHER, S.(1979) *Debate and Decision – Schools in a World of Change* London: World Studies Project

SCHOOLS COUNCIL (1981) *The Practical Curriculum* (Working Paper 70) London: Methuen Educational. This is a very helpful practical guide to curriculum planning.

6 Spreading the Load

However determined the head may be to succeed, however carefully the curriculum is planned, however conducive to creative learning the buildings are, the vital factor upon which the success of the school will depend is the nature and quality of the staff. No other single element has quite so much power to influence the way that a school develops. One of the central themes of this book is that a school is a human organization generating its own forces, creating its own tensions and striving to satisfy its needs. The nature of the authority structure which sets out to establish working relationships in an ordered way can itself be a powerful force within the school, determining whether the staff incline towards a positive dynamic or a negative one. An autocratic authority structure concentrates power over policy formation and decision-making in the hands of the head alone, whereas a more democratic structure attempts to disperse these vital functions between the various working members.

In attempting to establish a structure of shared decision-making the head will need to consider a number of factors:

1 the present authority/power structure in the school
2 the staff's perceptions of the head's role
3 the nature and extent of responsibility posts
4 staff attitudes towards power sharing
5 staff capacity for power sharing.

An important point which is often neglected when a more democratic approach to authority is being considered is that an increase in personal power and authority must be accompanied by an increasing obligation on the part of each individual to accept more responsibility. Just as the pursuit of rights and freedoms often fails to have regard for the concomitant duties, so the struggle for power is often one-sided.

In pursuing a participatory style of leadership the head will have to consider the sorts of roles and responsibilities that arise out of a more democratic approach to the running of the school. In this respect the most vital of the six management functions will be motivation and communication. The head needs to be a skilful motivator to get the best out of the staff, and success will to a large extent depend upon the assumptions he or she has made about teachers in general, and his or her colleagues in particular. One interesting theoretical construct which highlights the dangers of making wrong assumptions about people in organizations is Douglas McGregor's 'Theory X and Theory Y' (McGregor 1971).

Theory X: People dislike work and try to avoid it. They have to be bribed, coerced and controlled and even threatened with punishment to perform adequately. Most people wish to avoid responsibility and prefer being directed.

Theory Y: People do like work and don't have to be forced or threatened. If allowed to pursue objectives to which they are committed most people will work hard and not only accept responsibility, but consciously seek it.

If those who direct organizations proceed from Theory X then poor performance and a dislike of work are an inevitable outcome. If however individuals are encouraged to become involved in making decisions about the work they do, and in the way their organization develops, they will work more happily and more effectively. Clearly this is a somewhat simplistic view which conceals the fact that people are infinitely more complex than McGregor's dualistic analysis would seem to suggest. However, it does serve to emphasize that assumptions about people should be arrived at with caution. In terms of the authority structure in the school there is a direct relationship between head-teachers' assumptions about staff and their assumptions about the nature of headship. Heads who believe that it is neither desirable nor possible for teachers to participate in decision-making will regard their role as one of directing operations; whereas heads who consider it both desirable and necessary to involve colleagues in deciding how the school should develop will see themselves more as coordinators of activity than initiators of it.

To be a skilful motivator implies some knowledge of motivation itself. There is no shortage of theory and research on the subject, and study will repay the effort through increased understanding and insight. Many readers will be familiar with Maslow's motivation scheme which classifies human needs into a hierarchy. Another classic model, more relevant to the school situation, is that developed by Frederick Herzberg (in Pugh 1971). He found that in organizations one set of conditions — motivators — are likely to increase job satisfaction, while another set — hygiene factions — are likely to cause job dissatisfaction. The interesting discovery that Herzberg made was that there was no direct relationship between the two sets of factors. Those factors which motivate arise out of the nature of the job itself, whereas those which cause dissatisfaction are related more to the working environment.

Applying this to the school situation we have:

Motivators
Achievement: success in classroom tasks leading to a sense of achievement.
Recognition: the teacher is made aware, by the head particularly, that his or her work is valued, and is contributing to the success of the school.
Work itself: an enjoyment of teaching — the tasks undertaken and of the children themselves.
Responsibility: having a decision-making role, being the 'authority' in a curriculum area, being challenged.
Advancement: a sense of working towards a more challenging and responsible post.

Hygiene factors
Policy and administration: too many rules, regulations and procedures applying to staff. Difficulty of access to decision-makers.
Supervision: difficult relationship with head or deputy, 'bossy' attitudes causing frustration and anxiety.
Salary: poor and inadequate rewards for the work done.
Interpersonal relationships: poor staff morale, lack of cohesion, cliques, divisive attitudes.
Working conditions: lack of resources, poor facilities, lack of comfort.

Herzberg found from his research in industrial organizations that if motivation factors were low or even absent this did not result in job dissatisfaction, and that removing the hygiene factors did not result in an increase in job satisfaction.

The message is clear. In order to get the best out of staff a head has to devise ways of making colleagues' work sufficiently challenging and enriching to offer positive opportunities for individual fulfilment and professional development. One means of achieving this is delegation — which the dictionary defines as the entrusting of authority to a deputy or agent.

Heads in secondary schools are becoming increasingly familiar with the process. First, there has been a steady increase in the size of secondary schools so that most have more than one deputy head and a clear hierarchical structure based on the scales laid down by the Burnham Committee. Second, secondary schools work to a specialist curriculum representing a wide range of subjects, and teachers will generally have been recruited to exercize a specialist role. The

secondary head will have a specialism too, but cannot hope to demonstrate expertise in more than a quite narrow area of the curriculum,
and therefore has no choice but to delegate curriculum implementation to well-qualified heads of department. Third, secondary schools
break easily into sub-structures, either departmental ones based on
subjects, or pastoral ones based on year-groups or divisions. A final
point is that secondary schools generally provide more non-teaching
time for their senior staff, and it has become possible to separate the
purely management functions from the educational ones and to
develop expertise in the former.

The primary school is an altogether more intimate and informal
organization, and it might be thought that a more informal structure
would facilitate delegation, but this does not seem to be the case.
Writing in *The Role of the Head* (Peters 1976), A.A. Coulson refers to
various pieces of research which indicate that primary heads are
reluctant to involve their colleagues in policy making, staff supervision
and the management of innovation. In his article on the role of the
primary head, Coulson points to the persistence of paternalism, which
he identifies with the following characteristics:

1   Close personal identification of the head with the school – he
    thinks of it as 'his' school.
2   Close supervision by the head of every aspect of school life.
3   Close relationship between the personality of the head and the
    philosophy of the school.
4   Lack of confidence of the head in the abilities of teachers to work
    without supervision.

In noting these points Coulson raises two questions of fundamental
importance:

> However great the head's dedication, can he alone function competently as
> a leader in so many different fields – teacher training, management and
> administration, moral and social development, and so on? And all this with-
> out training or preparation except teaching experience. Surely a careful
> analysis of the traditional functions of headship is needed in order to
> determine which school matters, if any, he *must* decide and which can be
> left to others.

If the motivational function of leadership is to be successfully
carried out, and individual teachers are to find their various positions
both challenging and enriching, then delegation has to be regarded as
a high priority of headship. The central principle upon which a system
of delegation should be structured is that decisions should be made
as low down the organization as possible. Much can be delegated to
children. Most teachers would do well to examine the range of decisions that children are allowed to make for themselves. It is surprising,

for example, that in many classrooms children have considerable freedom to organize their own work, yet they have to seek permission to go
to the lavatory. Self discipline can only grow if it is given the opportunity to do so.

In seeking to establish the basic principles of delegation the head
will need to consider the following points:

1   delegation may involve a restructuring of the traditional authority
    relationships;
2   it implies an increase in the number of decisions that can be made
    without referral;
3   it depends for its success upon establishing relationships of trust;
4   it thrives on excellent communications.

It is important to make a distinction between authority structures
which are based on delegation, and those which masquerade as such.
The cynical advice is 'delegate nothing but blame'. Few heads would
go to this extreme, but there are perhaps more than a few who regard
delegation as an opportunity to allocate tasks they would rather not do
themselves. This is particularly true of delegation to deputies, and it
demonstrates a complete misunderstanding of what delegation is. My
earlier definition referred to the entrusting of authority, and this is the
key point. Delegation is not a matter of allocating tasks to a colleague,
but of enabling that teacher to be a policy maker, innovator, evaluator
and motivator, to be in charge of an area of responsibility. Teachers
achieve this delegated authority by demonstrating professional
ability, a capacity to exercise responsibility, in addition to an ability to
perform well and to make good decisions. Teachers recognize too they
have been entrusted with a role which reflects their abilities and
recognizes a high order of professional competence. Delegation is
clearly not for the faint-hearted, for it implies that the head is
prepared to take responsibility for the mistakes that colleagues may
take. As John Watts remarks, also in *The Role of the Head* (Peters
1976), the head should feel no guilt over being paid 'danger money'.

The question the head will need to ask is − which functions traditionally associated with headship is it unthinkable for me to delegate?
The longer the list, then the more autocratic the head.

The deputy head

If the role of head is difficult to define, that of the deputy is even more
problematical. Within our educational system the range and scope of
teachers' duties has never been the subject of prescription, and one of
the reasons why there is such divergence of role among deputies in
primary schools is that the precise nature of their work is left to the
individuals to work out. In practice, what deputies do ranges between

carrying out a few administrative chores at one extreme to a full association with school policy-making at the other.

Coulson's research into the role of the deputy head in the primary school reveals much that is of interest (Coulson and Cox 1975; Coulson 1976). He found the whole area of the deputy head's role surrounded with uncertainty and anxiety with the inevitable consequence of role frustration. In some schools the deputy head is regarded more as a senior teacher, with responsibility for the top junior class. Where particular duties were associated with the post they were invariably for requisitions and duty rotas. Coulson found it rare for a deputy to have a distinct area of authority separate from those of the head, and important decision-making by the deputy was only carried out in the absence of the head. One of the problems identified by Coulson's research is that in far too many cases being a deputy is an inadequate preparation for headship (Coulson and Cox 1975, 'What do deputies do?'):

> Despite his nominal status, the deputy is more likely to be overburdened with petty tasks and teaching than to be deeply involved with important issues concerning the school as a whole. This emphasis fails to make optimum use of the deputy's knowledge, skill and experience.

The vital factor, of course, is the attitude of the head to deputy headship. If a head is reluctant to regard the relationship with a deputy as a management partnership, then it is unlikely that the deputy will have a stimulating role, and will not therefore be able to contribute fully to the life and development of the school.

The head who is determined to undertake comprehensive delegation may still wonder how best to involve the deputy in the management of school affairs. Situational factors will be influential in determining both the deputy's role and how it is regarded by other members of staff. In some large primary schools the deputy has responsibility for school discipline and the supervision of staff duties. Such a role is often associated with a somewhat tough-minded 'no nonsense' approach to school life, and when a new head takes over it may prove very difficult to break down that traditional role definition and forge a new style of executive partnership.

Another interesting consideration arises out of the comparative philosophies, personalities and management styles of the head and deputy. Some heads are very conscious of this and deliberately set out to recruit a deputy who will complement their own qualities and thus bring a wider range of attitudes and ideas into the school. More perhaps go for the closest possible match to their own philosophy and personality in the belief that a doubling of the driving forces will help to bring about the changes they wish to see.

For the new head the establishment of a successful working relationship with the deputy will be a matter of some priority. The deputy may have spent the previous term as acting head. This taste of headship may well have increased the deputy's appetite for more responsibility, and it will be a poor head who does not seize this opportunity for establishing cooperative leadership. Some deputies have no desire to be heads but have considerable ability to perform the less senior role to a high standard. What often happens, however, is that a proficient deputy starts to seek promotion to headship. A deputy who has been in the school for some years will be of great value to a new head, and his or her experience, together with a knowledge of school developments, will be a vital resource when the new head begins the stock-taking exercise.

A training schedule for deputy heads

It is generally assumed that a deputy head is recruited as a potential head. Since primary heads are prone to the paternalism described by Coulson, and tend to undertake the majority of school management tasks themselves, few perhaps recognize their duty to help a deputy to prepare for eventual headship. The fact is that the deputy may be called upon at any moment to take over the running of the school, and it is a wise head who recognizes that possibility and makes plans for it. Perhaps one of the best ways to begin to consider the question of role definition for the deputy is in terms of a training schedule. Since there is very little in the way of systematic training for headship it is up to heads to compensate for this. The following checklist attempts to itemize some of the areas with which the deputy needs to become familiar. They can be categorized under three headings:

1   Areas of concern
Curriculum dimension:
    school plans and policies
    schemes of work
    evaluation procedures
    responsibility posts
    learning environment
    assemblies
Social dimension:
    clubs and activities
    breaktimes
    meal arrangements
    staff activities
    parent/teacher activities
Organizational dimension:
    class distribution
    room allocation
    resource management

school finance
governors
health and safety
routine administration
supervision of children
2   *Management skills*
planning
creating
communicating
motivating
organizing
controlling
3   *Leadership functions*
guiding, helping and explaining
working with and encouraging
being in front and leading

The deputy can be encouraged to consider the role of the head in terms of the key management functions, which can be applied to his or her own role too. Previous chapters have attempted to identify particular skills relevant to each of the functions, and put forward a framework to relate them to the decision-making process.

Clearly this is no mean task, and the schedule needs to be reworked into a programme which may well take up to nine terms to complete. While an intial overall plan will be necessary it will be important to have termly meetings in which precise objectives can be determined. The aims of this particular exercise are to:

1   provide an insight into the various management processes involved in the running of a primary school;
2   develop awareness and understanding of the roles of head, deputy, and teachers with special responsibility;
3   identify and consider the skills necessary to successful leadership;
4   practise and experience management and leadership tasks.

One factor that can inhibit the establishment of a sound relationship between head and deputy is the latter's teaching commitment. If the deputy is a full-time class teacher two problems arise: First, which role should have priority — that of teacher, or that of deputy? Second, the deputy is unable to be with the head while the latter is actually involved in the day-to-day business of being a head, so the head has the choice of either discussing what will be done before he or she does it, or of explaining what has been done afterwards. The key to success in this partnership is finding ways of minimizing these problems. Certainly regular briefing sessions are essential, and are probably better carried out daily rather than weekly. The purpose of the briefing is to outline the nature of current issues, to deal with incoming and outgoing correspondence, to discuss organizational matters and to monitor developing projects. The twenty minutes or so at the beginning of the school day are probably the best time, although some heads like to be available to staff and parents at this time.

To a large extent the role definition of the deputy will be derived from the training schedule. While such a programme is necessary and important it is essential that the deputy's role in the school is not regarded as a piecemeal responsibility. Like the head, the deputy has many roles to play in a lively and dynamic primary school. As Coulson has pointed out, (Coulson and Cox 1975, 'What do deputies do?') deputies in many schools have a collection of administrative tasks to perform, but seldom a special area of responsibility which they can call their own. In a sense the deputy is the senior scale-post holder in the school and should exercise a lively influence on the work of the school. Few deputies come to a post without previous experience as a scale-post holder, and it is vital that curriculum expertise is put to good use in the more senior post. Certainly it would suggest good management for the head and deputy to share the curriculum leadership of the school.

Various staffing structures are possible:

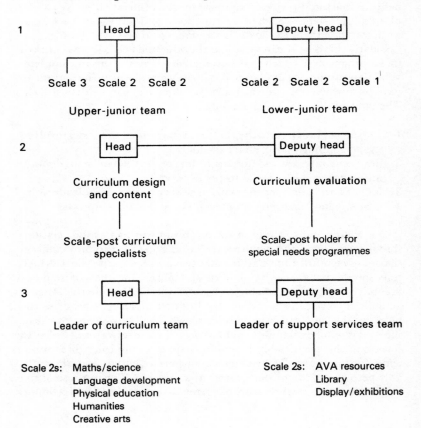

1

Head — Deputy head

Scale 3   Scale 2   Scale 2   Scale 2   Scale 2   Scale 1

Upper-junior team   Lower-junior team

2

Head — Deputy head

Curriculum design   Curriculum evaluation
and content

Scale-post curriculum   Scale-post holder for
specialists   special needs programmes

3

Head — Deputy head

Leader of curriculum team   Leader of support services team

Scale 2s: Maths/science   Scale 2s: AVA resources
           Language development   Library
           Physical education   Display/exhibitions
           Humanities
           Creative arts

Schools which are structured on year-groups also offer interesting leadership roles for both head and deputy:

4
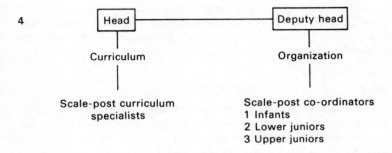

The possibilites for leadership sharing are considerable even in small schools, but in determining such structures it is important not to lose sight of the purposes of such an exercise, which are to:

1 Help the school work towards clearly-defined aims;

2 Make the best use of specialist expertise;

3 Provide support and guidance for all staff;

4 Facilitate school-based INSET and staff development;

5 Facilitate staff motivation and encourage job satisfaction;

6 Ensure continuity and progression in the curriculum.

A final quotation from Coulson (1976, 'Leadership Functions in Primary Schools') will serve to summarize the main points of this section:

As things stand, deputy headship often appears to be neither intrinsically satisfying, nor an adequate preparation for headship, since the aspiring deputy rarely has the opportunity to make the types of decision which will face him after promotion. The extension and elucidation of the deputy head's authority and discretion in school matters might enhance his satisfaction in his present post; it might also provide a more adequate preparation for further promotion. Moreover, greater delegation by heads, of authority as well as specific tasks, would help to erase the head's traditional image as an autocrat.

Scale posts

At the time of writing most primary schools are able to create posts on

Scale 2 while only schools in Group 5 and above are able to create those on Scale 3. Where it is possible to create a more hierarchical structure based on Scales 1, 2 and 3, consideration needs to be given to the nature of the differences between them; in other words the nature of the work differentials. If we assume that Scale 1 in the primary school encompasses all duties and responsibilities associated with full-time class teaching, then:

Scale 2 = Scale 1 + x
Scale 3 = Scale 1 + x + y or Scale 2 + y

The decision for the head concerns the values of x and y. Perhaps it should be said that the assumption made above about Scale 1 does not meet with universal agreement in primary schools. There has been a tendency to regard scale posts as rewards for good, or long, service; a sort of merit payment for past effort. It is important to establish the principle that extra allowances should involve extra duties and responsibilities; and consequently greater opportunities and challenges.

Few primary schools offer scope for a departmental structure and therefore other modes have to be established. One of the problems created by the Houghton Award of 1974 was the breaking down of the three-scale structure. In local authorities who awarded the maximum points available this created the somewhat ludicrous situation in some schools in Groups 4 and 5 of permitting all staff to be on Scale 2; and indeed gave some school more points than they could possibly use. Declining numbers on roll have compounded the problem and the Burnham Committee are faced with a considerable problem of scale reorganization if primary schools are to regain the opportunity of creating satisfactory staffing structures.

One of the problems created by this situation is that of equity. How can scale posts be allocated so that the distribution of duties and responsibilities is fair? Certainly the creation of more scale posts meant that heads were able to delegate more, but did so in a somewhat haphazard fashion. In one school a teacher on Scale 2 might have responsibility for a few administrative tasks while in another a teacher receiving similar Scale 2 payment may be designated a team leader with all the responsibilities which that brings. *Primary Education in England*, the survey by HM Inspectors of Schools (DES 1978) made the following point:

> In a quarter of the schools in the survey teachers with positions of curricular organizational responsibility were having a noticeable influence on the quality of the work in the school as a whole. In the remaining schools there was little evidence that the influence of teachers with curricular responsibilities spread beyond the work of their own classes.

Something more than 25 per cent effectiveness ought to be possible. One common problem is that new heads inherit a structure of scale posts and may feel it beyond their authority to attempt to change what has been long established. But providing it is handled constructively and sympathetically, a restructuring of scale-post allocations can be beneficial to each of the individuals concerned, and to the good of the school as a whole. This is not to suggest a change in the status of the teachers, but rather a revision and re-allocation of duties and responsibilities.

In the allocation of posts there are three models which can usefully be considered: curriculum model; organizational model; leadership model.

1 Curriculum model

Under this scheme all the teachers on Scales 2 and 3 have responsibility in a particular curriculum area. The HMI survey was very strong in its recommendation about this:

> 8.45 It is disappointing to find that the great majority of teachers with posts of special responsibility have little influence at present on the work of other teachers. Consideration needs to be given to improving their standing, which is the product of the ways in which the teachers with special posts regard themselves and also of the attitudes that other teachers have towards them.

> 8.46 It is important that teachers with special responsibility for, say, mathematics should, in consultation with the head, other members of staff and teachers in neighbouring schools, draw up the scheme of work to be implemented in the school; give guidance and support to other members of staff; assist in teaching mathematics to other classes where necessary; and be responsible for the procurement, within the funds made available, of the necessary resources for the teaching of the subject. They should develop acceptable means of assessing the effectiveness of the guidance and resources they provide, and this may involve visiting other classes in the school to see the work in progress.

The key to this issue is the head's capacity and willingness to delegate. Teachers will only become influential in their specialist role if the head is prepared to give them authority to act; and if other teachers will recognize and accept this. Let us consider a possible role definition for a teacher with special responsibility for mathematics:

1 To be responsible to the head for the design, implementation and evaluation of the mathematics programme throughout the school.
2 To be available to individual teachers for guidance and advice.
3 To convene meetings of teachers concerned to consider ways and means of developing the subject throughout the school.
4 To be responsible for submitting estimates for annual expenditure on mathematics and for coordinating the resource allocation.

5   To keep abreast of developments in primary school mathematics, and to be familiar with new publications, equipment and apparatus.
6   To liaise with the head of department of the secondary school, the advisers and the college of education.
7   To initiate and implement a system of evaluation for mathematics throughout the school.
8   To prepare reports for consideration by the staff and to prepare and present reports to the governors on the development of the subject.

One of the facts revealed by the HMI survey was that while responsibility for music was common in primary schools, responsibility for core curriculum subjects was not. Perhaps this is a reflection of the fact that teachers with subject responsibility are not given sufficient authority and status to perform the role adequately. Far too often responsibility for mathematics comes down to little more than the ordering of books and equipment. Until heads are prepared to create conditions in which teachers with responsibility in subject areas are given the authority to make policy as well as executive decisions, there is unlikely to be much improvement in this situation.

The curriculum model of scale-post allocation will work well if the teachers involved are sufficiently skilled and authoritative in their particular subject area. If the head feels that there is no one on the staff with an adequate blend of knowledge and experience of the subject to occupy the role, then another approach will be required.

2   Organizational model

This, like the previous model, works on the assumption that all members of staff have full-time responsibility for a class of children. The extra responsibility is associated with non-curriculum areas of school life, and directly related to a range of organizational functions such as:

1   stock control
2   resources
3   trips, visits, journeys
4   liaison with transfer schools
5   liaison with PTA
6   library.

Responsibilities such as the ones listed above are more in the nature of organizational support services than direct influences upon the curriculum of the school, but can add a special dimension to school life enabling it to operate both more efficiently and more effectively.

Stock control is often associated with the deputy head but there is no reason why it should be the prerogative of that position. A possible role definition for the teacher with responsibility for stock control might be:

1   To be responsible to the head (or the deputy) for stock purchase and allocation.
2   To work within the financial allocation to provide stationery and materials to meet the needs of the school.
3   To work with the secretary to establish and maintain a stock-control system that keeps the stockroom adequately supplied.
4   To monitor the usage of materials and to keep a check on quality and economy.
5   To undertake the ordering of stock and the checking of delivery notes, invoices and accounts.
6   To monitor the needs of the staff and advise on new products.
7   To prepare and present reports to governors.

Many primary schools are establishing resource centres where materials and equipments are made, stored, classified and distributed. In such circumstances it is vital to have a teacher responsible who can oversee and coordinate the whole operation. In view of the work involved it is also helpful to have the assistance of an ancillary assistant, and possibly the voluntary help of parents on a rota system.

Teacher with responsibility for the resource centre

1   To be responsible to the head for the maintenance and development of the resource centre.
2   To work within the financial allocation to provide a range of resources to meet the learning requirements of the school.
3   To organize and supervise the day-to-day running of the centre in co-operation with the ancillary assistant.
4   To create and maintain an efficient system of booking and allocating resources.
5   To monitor the needs of the staff and to keep them informed of new additions to the resource collection.
6   To be responsible for maintenance contracts on audio-visual equipment.
7   To establish and maintain adequate reprographic facilities to meet the needs of the staff.
8   To liaise with the LEA Resources Centres.
9   To prepare and present reports to governors.

School visits are such an integral part of primary school life these days that in a medium to large school it is useful to have a member of staff who can develop some expertise in the matter. Important issues of safety and supervision are involved and teachers should not be inhibited from using school visits by the rules and regulations associated with arranging them.

Teacher with responsibility for school visits

1 To be responsible to the head for policies and procedures associated with school visits.
2 To establish contact with places of interest in the locality which will be visited regularly — farms, churches, castles, museums, historical sites etc.
3 To maintain details of places to visit, names of personnel to contact, and regulations applicable.
4 To establish procedures for organizing:
    (a) short visits within the locality
    (b) full-day visits involving hired transport
    (c) residential visits in UK.
5 To advise on legal and insurance aspects of school visits.
6 To coordinate follow-up displays and exhibitions.
7 To prepare and present reports for governors.

It is very important that the transition of children from one school to another should be as smooth and as stress free as possible. One way to facilitate this is to give one of the teachers of the oldest children responsibility for it.

Teacher responsible for liaison with the secondary school

1 To be responsible to the head for organizing the transition of children to the secondary school.
2 To work with the secondary school in establishing satisfactory procedures for transfer.
3 To make regular visits to the secondary school and where possible arrange exchange visits of teachers.
4 To arrange the transfer of documents at the end of the academic year.
5 To advise parents about transfer and problems of choice, allocation and selection.
6 To prepare and present reports to governors.

In '*A New Partnership for our Schools*' (DES 1977) considerable importance was attached to the need for schools to establish good relationships with its parent body. In a school which has dynamic parent/teacher activity there is much scope for a post of responsibility to be associated with it.

Teacher with responsibility for parent liaison

1 To be responsible to the head for maintaining relationships with

the Parent/Teacher Association.

2   To make arrangements for meetings of the PTA.

3   To liaise regularly with the chairperson of the PTA and service the channels of communication.

4   To monitor and represent the views of the staff not involved in committee work of the PTA.

5   To make contact with new parents.

6   To prepare and present reports to the governors.

All of these posts are concerned with establishing and maintaining an efficient and happy organization. The work involved is challenging and demanding and likely to develop organizational skills. Although not directly concerned with the curriculum these posts will, if carried out to a high level of performance, so contribute to the general life of the school that there will be a marked and beneficial effect upon the curriculum work. Much will depend upon the head; if he or she prefers to undertake the curriculum leadership then colleagues will be more likely to respond to the organizational tasks outlined above.

3 Leadership model

This is perhaps more applicable to the larger primary school. It covers a range of responsibilities which can loosely be considered to have a co-ordinating function. Many primary schools have a teacher who is designated as head of the infant department. This involves a responsibility for the work of other teachers and consequently requires management skills. There is no higher responsibility than that for the work of others, and it is curious that in many primary schools teachers with such leadership roles can have a higher level of responsibility than the deputy head, yet receive considerably less in the way of salary.

In some large junior schools teachers are divided into teams. One member is designated as the team leader and given responsibility for coordinating activities, convening meetings and liaising with the head. The role need not always involve a supervisory element but does imply a leadership function. In a three-form entry school there may be a team leader for each age-range of children, and in large open-plan schools some teachers may lead a team in a particular area of the school.

Another responsibility role which comes within this category is that of working with probationary teachers and students on school practice. Such a post can offer a challenging and stimulating role for a teacher and can provide some excellent training in management skills.

Teacher with responsibility for probationary teachers and students.

1   To be responsible to the head for the guidance of probationary teachers and students.

2   To work in consultation with the head, deputy and the governors
    in the appointment of probationary teachers.
3   To be responsible for arrangeing pre-interview visits to the school
    and for showing candidates round the school and introducing
    them to the staff.
4   Following appointment, to liaise with the successful student and
    arrange visits to the school.
5   To work in consultation with the head and deputy to devise and
    supervise a programme of introduction for the probationary
    teachers.
6   To prepare and present reports to the governors.

In practice it is unlikely that a school will adopt only one of these
models. Where curriculum, organizational and leadership posts of
responsibility coexist it is important that equity is established and that
there is a clear difference between Scale 2 and Scale 3. Generally
speaking leadership responsibilities would seem to demand a Scale 3
post.

One question that concerns some heads, and indeed many teachers,
is that of role conflict. This can be overcome to a great extent by
formulating with the teachers concerned clear role definitions along
the lines of the examples quoted above. What is vitally important is
that all members of staff should have copies of these, so that areas of
responsibility can be easily identified and the risk of conflict considerably reduced. The role definition should make clear the nature of the
delegation involved, and specify those areas where the teacher has
authority to make decisions.

The head can help to give posts of responsibility the status they
deserve by not making decisions on behalf of a colleague. Teachers
who approach the head with a problem should be encouraged to take
it to the teacher in whose area of responsibility the problem lies.
Delegation involves a deliberate reduction in the head's own decision-
making role. If teachers are to grow in confidence in their roles the
head must resist the temptation to act for them.

The relationship between the head and a teacher with delegated
authority is a crucial one. The head needs to have confidence in the
colleague's ability to fulfil the requirements of the special role, but also
needs to recognize that support and encouragement will be necessary.
Status is measured by the extent to which the head is prepared to leave
things to colleagues, and also by the recognition of that fact by the rest
of the staff.

In attempting to establish relationships of trust heads will need to be
in a state of continual consultation with colleagues, both to satisfy
their own need for information and knowledge, and also so that a sense
of corporate teamwork is encouraged. In a flourishing and dynamic
team there will be an inevitable blurring of the edges of role definitions, and providing that communications are good this will serve the

interests of the school as a whole, reflecting that the teachers, in pursuit of commonly-agreed aims, are working for, and with each other.

It is very important that role definitions for posts of responsibility are not regarded as immutable. On the other hand neither should they be considered merely transitory. It is a useful practice to submit role definitions to annual review. Not only does this allow an individual an opportunity to modify a role definition in the light of changed circumstances, but also to consider the nature of the role itself. Sometimes a change of responsibility can provide a new and much needed challenge, and at the same time bring new thinking to an area of school life which may be in need of some development. This annual review should not be regarded as an 'all change', but rather as a time for taking stock, responding to new developments and seeking fresh solutions to old problems. A good way for the head to handle this review is through a series of appraisal interviews. Part of the previous year's interview should have been the setting of objectives for the ensuing twelve months. These can be discussed and evaluated in the interview, new objectives set and the role definition adjusted if necessary. Following the series of interviews new objectives and role definitions will need to be documented and circulated so that everyone is aware of the changes. Teamwork and mutual support can only exist when everyone is clear what everyone else is trying to do.

In a school which operates a participatory decision-making system, the staff as a whole should be involved in this annual review of responsibility posts. An earlier chapter discussed the desirability of an annual report following the decision-making body's evaluation of its previous year's efforts. Role adjustment is closely associated with this. New posts of responsibility may be needed to accompany new school goals, and where extra posts are not available they can be created by redefining old ones. Close consultation with the governors is desirable during this exercise.

One of the implications of falling rolls in primary schools is that job mobility in the teaching profession is becoming considerably reduced. As a result there are fewer senior positions available, and unless the Burnham structure undergoes some change many primary teachers will have to be satisfied for a very much longer period with a Scale 2 post. During the early 1970s teachers working their way up the promotional ladder were on the move every two or three years, and it was not uncommon for headships to be changing hands every three or four years. In the changed circumstances of the late 70s and early 80s the annual review of scale posts takes on a more fundamental purpose — that of providing the opportunity for a teacher to maintain a steady professional development through gaining new and wider experience within the same school.

Notwithstanding this situation, teachers with responsibility posts will leave the school from time to time, and the question of replacement arises. Two choices are possible:

1   to recruit a teacher who can fill a predetermined specialist
     vacancy;
2   to look for a good all-round class teacher and sort out the respon-
     sibility later.

Since a primary school derives its strength from the skills and qualities
of its class teachers, it is important to give general teaching ability
priority over specialist skill. It is perhaps easier to encourage a good
class teacher to develop a specialism than to get a specialist to become
a good general practitioner. Second, the scale-post allowance represents quite a small element of the teacher's remuneration. Scale posts
provide opportunities for good general teachers to develop specialist
skills, and to begin to take on a more responsible and authoritative role
in the school.

References

COULSON, A.A (1976) Leadership Functions in Primary Schools
    Educational Administration, 5,1
COULSON, A.A and COX, M. (1975) What do deputies do? *Education
    3–13*, 3, 2
MCGREGOR, D. (1971) Rensis Likert and Douglas McGregor in D.S.
    Pugh, D.J. Hickson, C.R. Hinings (eds) *Writers on Organizations*
    . Harmondsworth: Penguin
DES (1977) *A New Partnership for Our Schools* (The Taylor Report)
    London: HMSO
DES (1978) *Primary Education in England: A survey by HM Inspectors
    of Schools* London: HMSO
PETERS, R.S. (1976) *The Role of the Head* London: Routledge &
    Kegan Paul.
I UGH, D.S. (ed) (1971) *Organizational Theory* Harmondsworth:
    Penguin

7   Appointing Staff

There are few tasks which the head undertakes that are as important and as far reaching as the selection and appointment of new members of staff. It is perhaps surprising that some heads will agonize over a decision to purchase an expensive piece of equipment but set about filling a staff vacancy rather casually. Surprising, because a mistake over a piece of equipment can be absorbed by most schools but a mistake over the selection of a teacher may bring problems to a school which will continue for many years. Few heads perhaps consider the nature of the investment they are undertaking when an appointment to the teaching staff has to be made. At current salary levels, a teacher appointed on Scale 2 for five years represents a cost of about £40,000. Teachers are the most expensive resource a school has, and it is vital that they are wisely selected.

The decline in primary school rolls was referred to in the previous chapter. Unless there is considerable readjustment of pupil-teacher ratios there will be a corresponding decline in the number of primary school teachers, and consequently teachers will be spending longer periods of time in the schools to which they are appointed. This, combined with the problems of the property market and an inflationary economy, has severely reduced teacher mobility. There is a much greater reluctance to change jobs − even to seek promotion − if this will mean moving house, and while this has brought a much needed staff stability to schools it has also meant that selection has to be handled even more carefully.

Each local education authority has its own particular procedure for the appointment of staff, and practices vary considerably. The two extremes of approach would seem to be:

1   The local authority handles the entire appointment process with

no involvement of the head.

2   The whole procedure is delegated to the head.

Most heads will be involved in a procedure which lies somewhere between these two. Teachers contemplating seeking a headship appointment in a different authority would be wise to seek out the details of the appointing procedure they would be required to operate.

Procedures for the appointment of staff are established in the Rules of Government, and this should be studied with care to determine the extent to which governors and the head are involved. Generally speaking in county and controlled schools, assistant teachers are appointed, employed and dismissed by the local authority, but some aspects of the selection system are delegated to the governors who are required to work in consultation with the head. In aided schools, although the local authority determines whether an appointment should be made, and pays the salary, the governing body is responsible for selecting and employing assistant teachers.

A number of authorities, recognizing the key role of the head, have devolved a great deal of their powers so that the working procedures for appointing staff are the result of close consultation between the head and the governors. I can see no plausible reason why a head should be denied an important executive and consultative role in the selection and appointment of teaching and non-teaching staff in the school.

For the rest of this chapter I have made the following working assumptions:

1   The head is responsible for conducting the preselection aspects of the appointing procedure, including:
     (a) the wording of the advertisement
     (b) the preparation of 'details on request'
     (c) receiving the applications
     (d) arranging for applicants to visit the school.
2   The governors, in consultation with the head, are responsible for selecting candidates and recommending their appointment to the local education authority. These responsibilities to include:
     (a) the drawing up of the short list
     (b) arranging and conducting interviews
     (c) notifying unsuccessful candidates.

In many authorities an adviser for primary education is involved in the appointing procedure. This can be very helpful to the head and governors by bringing a wider perspective of the educational scene to the needs of a particular school.

Since a sense of cohesion among members of staff is a vital attribute of the successful school, any appointments should reflect this and attempt to preserve, and indeed improve, the subtle but crucial human dynamics which make for a happy and efficient organization. The head is in the best position to appreciate these human considerations and to judge whether a candidate has the personality and skills which can be easily assimilated by the working team. If the head is denied the key role in the appointing procedure then the chances of making wise and beneficial appointments are very much reduced.

There are many reasons why a head can be faced with the need to appoint a new member of staff. An increase in the roll can create a vacancy, and perhaps also the need for a new class to be formed. Routine resignations, either because of promotions or retirements, also create the need for replacement. The one causing heads the most concern is that of maternity leave, which in most instances is a delayed resignation. The virtue of the legislation is not in doubt, but in terms of providing satisfactory staffing it can cause serious problems. It can mean that a class of children has three different teachers in the course of one academic year — the teacher who takes the maternity leave, the temporary replacement, and the eventual full-time replacement. If a post of responsibility is being vacated then the work associated with it cannot be taken over by the temporary replacement who is only on Scale 1. Clearly the more flexible the staff, the easier these problems are to minimize.

Assessing the vacancy

The first task for the head who receives a teacher's resignation is to assess the nature of the vacancy and to reflect upon its significance to the work of the school as a whole. This is more than a mere inward expression of pleasure or regret that a particular colleague is leaving the school; it is a more comprehensive attempt to recognize the gap that will need to be filled. Clear objective thinking is needed. An assessment sheet (see Fig.7.1, p. 104) not only directs the head's thinking in a specific way, but can also help in the later stages of recruitment. The sheet is concerned more with the departing teacher than with the replacement. It is an attempt to identify a range of skills, abilities and qualities that will be lost to the school.

Essentially completing this sheet will help to identify the professional and personal qualities that the departing teacher brought to the school. The head needs to be clear about the basic principle of selection which is to achieve the best possible match between the potential skills and qualities of a candidate and the needs of the school. Not only does this remind us of the two essential aspects of organizational life — people and purpose — but it also serves to identify the two key elements of the appointment procedure — assessing the qualities of applicants and relating them to the needs of the school.

Having decided what sort of gap the departing teacher will create in the school, the next stage is to decide what sort of person should be

	Skills	Qualities	Experience	Special factors
Class teacher				
Scale 2 responsibilities				
Personal				

Figure 7.1   Vacancy assessment sheet

sought to fill it. It may well be that a different set of qualities are necessary to promote or maintain healthy staff relationships; or a different
set of skills in order to stimulate innovation in a particular area of the
curriculum. The first task for the head is to consider the needs of the
school. A distinction needs to be made between current and immediate needs, and those related to longer-term school developments. It
could be that the immediate need is to restore a sense of stability to a
class which has been subjected to a series of supply teachers since their
class teacher's resignation. A good class teacher of some experience,
with sympathy and understanding of the predicament the class is in,
will certainly help to restore the situation. But such a teacher should
also have been appointed because of a potential to assist the realization
of longer-term school goals, whether they be concerned with
mathematics or team-teaching. These needs, once identified, should
be listed as a series of objectives for the appointment. Efficiency is
often best served by having a standard form to fill in (see Fig. 7.2,
p. 105). This can be kept with all the papers relating to the appointment and serves to act as a constant reminder of the qualities being
sought. It is surprising how important this is, for it is quite easy to
rationalize the needs of the school in the light of exceptional
recommendations among applicants. It could be tempting to demote
the long-term aim of developing art and design in the school in favour
of a brass band because one applicant is an ex-member of Black Dyke
Mills!

In attempting to define further the qualities being looked for, the
vacancy assessment sheet can again be used. This systematic approach
will assist considerably the more complex later stages of the procedure.

Having made decisions about:

Reason for appointment:		
Scale:	Class:	Age of children:

Special requirements:

1

2

3

4

5

6

7

8

9

10

Figure 7.2 Appointment objectives form

1 the immediate needs of the school,
2 the long-term needs of the school,
3 the qualities required of the new teacher,

the next stage is to seek out those who will satisfy these demands. This is usually done by placing an advertisement in the educational press, although in many LEAs vacancies are being filled by redeployment and transfer with only senior posts being advertised. Unlike advertisements for key personnel in industrial organizations, which can extend to many column inches, those for teachers in primary schools are usually couched in the briefest terms, as the following examples illustrate:

Required for April or earlier:
Long Lane JMI School   Roll 348
Experienced junior teacher
Please state interests   Scale 1

Somewhat better is:

Down County Primary School
Roll 100
Applications are invited from suitably qualified persons for the
post of ASSISTANT TEACHER for General Subjects. Musical
ability desirable. Enthusiastic teacher prepared to enter fully
into life of school. Scale 1 post. The successful applicant will
be expected to take up the appointment in April.

Almost good enough is:

Required for April:
Deer Edge JMI School, Deer Lane, SOUTHSIDE
Roll 450
Experienced teacher, initially for lower juniors
Scale 2 or 3.
Scale 3 post available for an enthusiastic, efficient teacher,
able to combine special responsibilities for Maths and Science
with assistance in Athletics, Football, Swimming, possibly
Chess, and willing to undertake substantial extra-mural
activities.

With such restrictions on the number of words available it is very difficult to provide an indication to would-be applicants of the particular
qualities being sought and the level of qualifications and experience
expected. This is a pity because one of the important functions of an
advertisement is to narrow the field of applicants. A great deal of time,
money and effort is wasted by teachers applying for posts for which
they are clearly unsuitable. This is an unhappy situation, both for
applicants and for heads. Often the head will have to reject applications merely because the requirements of the job were not made clear.
 The device that has been invented to minimize this confusion is the
ubiquitous details on request. This provides the head with an opportunity to spell out in some detail the sort of applicant wanted. Far
too often, however, the details turn out to be little more than a brief
description of the school buildings and the number of children on
roll. Such details should furnish enough information to enable an
interested teacher to make a decision whether or not to apply for the
post. The following information should always be provided:

1 Name and address of school.
2 Title of vacant post.
3 Designation and group of school, number on roll and number of
   staff.
4 Description of buildings
5 Outline of school philosophy, organization and curriculum.
6 Extra curriculum activities.
7 Requirements of the post.
8 Scale-post responsibilities.

9   Procedure for applying, with projected time scale.
10 Enclosures — school handbook, map of catchment area, staff list etc.

In order to administer the appointment process efficiently it is important to work out a systematic procedure. Much of the routine work will be carried out by the school secretary. It is helpful, and usually essential, to have a checklist to ensure efficiency.

APPOINTMENTS CHECKLIST		
TASK 1 Obtain written resignation	DATE DONE	BY (initials)
2 Inform staffing at County Hall		
3 Inform Chairman of governors of advert		
4 Inform County Hall wording		
5 Prepare details for applicants		
6 On receipt of inquiries: (a) enter details on inq. list (b) send details (c) file correspondence		
7 On receipt of applications: (a) acknowledge (b) enter details on list (c) file application		
8 Shortlist: (a) send for references (b) prepare schedules (c) invitations to interview		
9 Following interview: (a) inform candidates not called (b) confirm appointment with C.H. (c) forward details to C.H. (d) letters to interview candidates		

Figure 7.3   Appointments checklist

Some local authorities do not have a very happy record of dealing with applicants for teaching posts. When appointments are dealt with centrally the whole process takes on the complexion of a lottery. The great advantage of being able to deal with appointments at the individual school level is that it becomes possible to treat applicants with the courtesy and consideration they deserve and should have a

right to expect. There seems to be a general assumption that authorities are doing the teaching profession a favour by advertising teaching
posts. In reality the opposite is true. By offering themselves for
appointment to a vacant post, applicants are making it possible for
schools to overcome their staff shortages. Any authority should be
grateful that teachers go to the trouble of offering themselves for consideration for a post. In my experience applications, while not always
technically of high quality, are always gracious and polite. The same
cannot be said of the peremptory, sometimes curt replies that many
applicants receive from county halls. Candidates should always be
thanked with sincerity for applying, and be informed with regret if
they have not been successful.

It has become more usual in recent years for teachers interested in a
vacant post to ask to visit the school before committing themselves to
an application. This makes very good sense, for it is essential that the
person appointed should feel attracted by the school, both in terms of
its educational philosophy and practice, as well as its organizational
dynamics. Telephone inquiries are also becoming more common,
particularly if the advertisement has only given the merest hint of the
nature of the post. Either the inquirer can be sent a copy of the details,
or if they are local can be invited to visit the school, during the school
day if this can be arranged. A willingness to do this is an indication of
the seriousness of interest being shown. The visit of a potential
candidate has two clear benefits. First, it allows a far more fundamental insight into the working of the school, and second it provides
an opportunity for the head and colleagues to meet a range of potential candidates.

Visits should whenever possible be arranged in school time. An
empty school is always interesting to walk around, but is very difficult
to assess, particularly in terms of the elusive 'atmosphere' which some
teachers seem to have an instinctive feel for. A full day visit is the ideal,
but this is rarely possible. What is important is that the visit itself
should not be merely a conducted tour. It is worth considering who is
the best person to show interested teachers round. As a general rule it
is probably someone on the same scale as that of the post being
advertised. The head is often regarded as the obvious person to
perform the duty, but there are good reasons why the task should be
delegated. First it is better for the visitor to get a teacher's view of the
school, including a view of the head. Second, the visitor will feel more
relaxed, notice more of what is going on and ask more questions.
Third, it is good delegation.

Visits should not be casual affairs. As far as time permits the visitor
should have the opportunity to:

1   see the building inside and out
2   observe the children and staff at work
3   talk with the children

4   meet the staff, preferably during a break or the lunch hour
5   meet the teacher who is leaving, and the particular class the
    successful candidate will be teaching
6   talk with the head.

At the end of each visit the head should document impressions. A
head who works closely with colleagues will be anxious for them to
realize that the appointing exercise is one of selecting a colleague, and
will wish to take their views into consideration. The impressions of the
teacher conducting the visit will be very important, and the staff,
having had an opportunity to consider a possible colleague, should be
encouraged to express their impressions.

Eventually some applications will arrive at the school. These should
be processed by the secretary and then kept until the closing date is
reached. Even if there is only one application it is essential that a
strategy for dealing with written applications is worked out and
applied. The main purpose of this is to narrow the field to a shortlist of
candidates who on paper satisfy the requirements of the job. There is
no universal formula for this strategy, but one approach is to select a
range of factors which are likely to influence decisions about suitability. These can be set out in the form of a schedule for easy reference (see Fig. 7.4).

Apart from the important information they contain, applications
are an interesting phenomenon in themselves. Badly-made photo-
copies, perfumed notepaper, lengthy monographs on educationl philosophy, chatty notes about weekend rambles, heroic citations about

Name	Age	Scale	Length of exp.	No. of schools	Qualifications	In-Service	x

Figure 7.4   Schedule of applicants

life at the chalk face – all these, together with numerous excellent applications, conspire to make the act of selection a fascinating, if daunting, task. One head I know commits to the waste bin immediately any application written on lined paper, or more than two pages long, or which fails to enclose a stamped addressed envelope.

It has already been stated that appointment procedures vary from authority to authority. This is particularly so in the use of application forms. It is still possible to find some forms which require information about 'O' level grades and some which provide vast spaces for training qualifications but only a tiny area for any further information the candidate may wish to offer. A number of authorities, recognizing the limitations imposed by forms, invite applications in letter form. As Cyril Poster (1976) points out in *School Decision-Making*: 'Letters of application, however brief, will always contain the seeds of a useful discussion at interview.' Perhaps the one useful function of a form is that it facilitates the communication of basic information. Where no forms are provided wise applicants enclose a curriculum vitae which conveys the essential information, and also indicates something of the applicant's assessment of what is important and what merely trivial.

In order to make a satisfactory shortlist the evidence has to be assessed. The vital documents will be the application form, or curriculum vitae, and the supporting letter. Testimonials are less popular than they used to be, but a few authorities still require them. There are various ways of dealing with written applications. One is to have three piles to sort them into:

1   reject – obviously unsuitable
2   possible – largely suitable
3   probable – suitable

Another way is by a gradual process of elimination until only the number required for interview purposes is left. Whatever method is chosen it is obvious that some selection criteria have to be applied. The appointment schedule illustrated above specifies the key factors which constitute suitability for the post in question, what now remains is to attach some system of loading to the factors themselves. This raises another fundamental issue of selection. In seeking to fill a vacant post, does the head:

1   invite the six most suitable applicants for an interview and then appoint the most promising of those, or
2   only invite for interview candidates who on paper fulfil the requirements of the job, and then recommend for appointment the candidate who most closely matches these requirements?

Theoretically the second is the only feasible approach, yet far too often appointing bodies make fundamental errors of selection. A number of reasons may explain this:

1   The requirements of the job were not adequately determined.
2   The shortlisting process was not systematically conducted.
3   Poor interviewing techniques were employed.
4   There was little attempt to assess how closely the 'best' candidate
    came to satisfying the requirements formulated.

It is crucial to decide how far short of ideal the appointing body are prepared to go. Far too often the pressure to appoint — because of cost, resignation dates or availability of appointing panel — is so strong that sometimes candidates who fall below the threshold of suitability are appointed. The decision not to appoint is often a difficult one, but sometimes has to be taken in the best interests of both school and candidate. A careful and systematic process of shortlisting will go some way to ensure that unsuitable candidates do not get to the interview stage.

The various factors identified in the appointment schedule need to be weighted in a way which recognizes their comparative importance. Perhaps the best way to do this is to have some application assessment sheets duplicated (see Fig. 7.5).

Name of applicant			
Factor	Detail	Weighting	Score

Figure 7.5   Application assessment sheet

A sheet can be completed for each candidate as the application is scrutinized, and a score given for each factor. Total scores can be compared and the top half dozen or so assessed in terms of their interview suitability. Further weighting can be applied by fixing a minimum score for those factors which are of overriding importance.

Before the decision about the interview list is made, there are further consultations to arrange. Certainly the chairman of governors will need to be involved and may be keen to see all the applications. It is worth going to some pains to explain to the governing body how the assessment of applications is carried out, and to give reasons for the criteria which have been applied.

The deputy head too should be involved at all stages of the appointment procedure. Not only is it necessary training and experience for headship, but the deputy's view of the needs of the school and the personal factors involved will be an important contribution to the final decision. If there are year or departmental heads, and the vacant post falls within the area of their responsibility, then obviously they should take part in the procedure as well.

There is no virtue in hurrying the shortlisting exercise, and to avoid this some careful and detailed planning is necessary. Upwards of three people will need to read the applications, and then a meeting should be convened to decide on the candidates to be invited for interview. It is best to plan this early in the process in order to give the governors plenty of notice and to avoid that sense of panic which sometimes accompanies the appointing process, particularly when there is a problem of deadlines for resignations.

There seems to be an assumption that a shortlist should consist of six candidates. The reason usually offered in support of this number is that six candidates are about the maximum an interviewing panel can comfortably cope with in one session. Additionally, it is sometimes suggested that six candidates offer a reasonably wide range of skills and qualities. This point however conflicts with one of the main aims of selection — that of bringing to the interview stage only those candidates who have demonstrated competence in a particular range of skills. If there are only three candidates who on paper satisfy the shortlisting requirements, then only three should be interviewed. There can be no virtue in calling a candidate who in theory would not be appointed. Much will depend upon the number of applicants satisfying the shortlisting requirements, and the difference between their comparative strengths. Certainly no candidate should ever be invited to interview merely to make up the numbers.

Once the shortlist has been decided the process takes on a more personal quality. It is important to remember that the school is now inviting a number of applicants to submit themselves to quite severe examination of their professional and personal qualities. Courtesy and consideration for candidates is not always of the highest order when teachers are appointed and many can tell quite horrific stories of what they have been subjected to. Proceeding to the interview stage not only raises the hopes of the candidates, but presents something of a crisis in their personal life. Success in the interview can mean the satisfaction of an ambition, but also the prospect of domestic and professional upheaval. Failure, on the other hand, brings disappointment and often a blow to self confidence and pride. Those charged with the responsibility for making decisions about appointments should be sensitive to these human factors and do all within their power to make the interview process as free from discomfort as possible.

Before interviews take place, it is usual to take up references of the shortlisted candidates. Most teachers give their current head as the first referee, and he or she should always be approached for a report. Some schools supply a special form inviting the referee to make comments about the candidate's suitability, character and punctuality. Such forms have something of the limitation of application forms. Much better is a personal letter to the referee asking for information specific to the post on offer. A copy of the details for candidates should be enclosed and any further information which may help the referee to give a relevant report. Main references should always be sought in writing despite the current tendency for the telephone to be used.

An invitation to an interview should also be in the form of a personal letter. This should contain the following information:

1   where to come
2   time to arrive
3   estimated length of interview
4   people involved in the interview
5   programme of events, e.g. look round school, lunch etc.
6   transport details, e.g. parking facilities, buses, trains, etc.
7   expenses
8   how and when the decision will be made.

The letter should also ask candidates to confirm that they will be attending. At least two weeks notice should be given.

The interviews need the same careful planning that has been applied to the earlier stages of the process. The composition of the panel will have to be decided upon and those taking part informed of the time and date, and furnished with the necessary papers – copies of forms, letters of application and summary schedules. A preinterview meeting will need to be arranged so that the interview strategy can be discussed and final details sorted out.

The location and the setting for the interviews has to be considered. It seems fairly standard practice in education for all the candidates for a teaching appointment to be called to the school at the same time, to be interviewed in turn for about twenty minutes, and then to wait together until deliberations are completed and the selection made. The successful candidate is called back to be offered the post, leaving the others to join in some forced bonhomie before they depart to ponder why Mrs X was offered the job and they were not. There are many faults with this approach. First, there can be no justification for calling a candidate to an interview at 9.00 a.m. and asking him or her to wait for two hours while other candidates are seen. Second, there are some experiences which are best faced alone, and going through the interview process is probably one of them.

It is quite simple to arrange interviews in such a way that candidates arrive at intervals. After the interview the candidates are free to make their way home having made arrangements with the head to be contacted about the outcome. This is a much more civilized way of treating candidates and gives their comfort and well-being the consideration it deserves. A telephone call to the unsuccessful candidates can be more informal and considerate than a general announcement to a crowded room, and also presents the opportunity of thanking candidates for applying for the post and submitting themselves to an interview.

Such a system is also much easier to manage. The only rooms required are a waiting-room and the interview room itself. Choice of rooms is important. The interview room should be comfortable and conducive to private conversation. The chairs should be arranged in an informal way and there should be no hiding behind desks. Direct sunlight should be avoided. It is necessary to eliminate the possibility of interruption, either from children knocking on the door or from telephone calls. Easy chairs help to make the proceedings relaxed but excessive informality can put candidates at a disadvantage and should be avoided. It should always be made clear where the candidate is expected to sit, and a glass of water provided.

The staff of the school should know of the plans for the interview. Children too need to be aware of what is going on. A summary of events should be posted on the staff noticeboard referring to the candidates involved, the times of their interviews and special arrangements made necessary as a result of members of staff being required on the interviewing panel.

The school secretary should be briefed about the day's events and made responsible for looking after the welfare of visiting candidates. Someone should be on hand to receive the candidates as they arrive — the member of staff whose responsibility it was to show candidates round the school would be the best person to do this — and show them to the waiting-room. Cloakroom facilities should be put at the candidate's disposal and refreshment provided if needed. Soon after the candidate has arrived the head should join him or her for a brief informal meeting to go over the details of how the interview will be conducted, who will be involved, and how the outcome will be managed. The secretary can deal with travelling expenses.

Interviews should never be conducted without a carefully worked-out plan. It should contain:

1   An agreed procedure for conducting the interview — who will make the introductions, who will show the candidate out etc.
2   An agreed list of questions — all candidates should be asked

questions on the same main issues.
3 An agreed list of items on which judgments are required.
4 An agreed assessment procedure.

Each member of the interviewing panel will require:

1 a copy of the application form or letter
2 a copy of the application assessment sheet
3 a copy of the 'job specification'
4 a blank assessment sheet

The interview assessment sheet (see Fig. 7.6) serves a number of purposes. First, it focuses the panel's attention by listing the items on which eventual judgment will be made. Second, it provides a convenient format for making notes. Third, it allows scoring. The design of the sheet will be determined by the nature of the post on offer.

Candidate's name:		
Appearance and manner		1 2 3 4 5
Professional attitudes		1 2 3 4 5
Management potential		1 2 3 4 5
Personality		1 2 3 4 5
Special responsibility potential		1 2 3 4 5
Overall impression		1 2 3 4 5

Figure 7.6 Interview assessment sheet (the categories will vary according to the precise nature of the vacant post)

Other planning details will include the ordering of questions and questioners and the length of the interview. The interview should fall into four distinct phases:

1   introduction
2   establishing rapport
3   acquiring information
4   conclusion

It is best for the head to fetch the candidate from the waiting-room, and to introduce him or her to each member of the panel. Warmth and friendliness are more quickly established if the introductions include a handshake. The first objective is for the panel and the candidate to establish rapport. The member of the panel most skilful at this should handle the first five minutes of the interview. A useful opening gambit is to look for a common link to give a start to the conversation. This can usually be picked out from the application. Candidates gain confidence from the fact that the panel are familiar with their professional history.

Once rapport is established and the candidate has had some opportunity to warm up on questions of a fairly general nature, the main substance of the interview can commence. This is the stage when the candidate is invited to respond to the questions which have been specifically designed to elicit enough information to enable eventual judgments to be made. Responses to the questions can be assessed on a five-point scale. It may be necessary to press the candidate for more information, or to follow up questions. Probing may put the candidate under some pressure but the interview should never be allowed to deteriorate into an interrogation. Early on it may be necessary to help the candidate over a difficult silence but eventually he or she must be left to cope. While there is obviously something wrong with the interview if the candidate does not do most of the talking it is sometimes helpful to have some summary or reflection from one of the interviewers. Candidates' aptitude in the interview can provide some indication of how they measure up to a stressful situation, but it is dangerous to place too much reliance on mere interview ability. The questioning should be designed to help candidates give pointers to their:

1   ability to do the job
2   achievements in present and previous jobs
3   relationships with colleagues
4   teaching style and how it relates to the school model
5 . potential to develop
6   capacity for self evaluation

By getting candidates to talk about their thoughts, ideas, attitudes and feelings the panel should be able to gain an insight into these vital aspects of professional life.

When the main questions have been covered the final stage of the interview is reached. Questions now become more factual and specific and biographical details can be checked and also information about possible future arrangements. It is customary, and considerate, to ask the candidates if there is any further information they would like to volunteer, or to ask questions of the panel. Finally, the candidate is thanked and shown back to the waiting-room. The secretary can see to any final matters and then see the candidate off the premises.

When all the candidates have been interviewed the panel must make their decision. During the ensuing discussion data collected during the interviews is reviewed, potential compared and judgments made. Some panels approach this part of the process by taking an immediate vote to see how the ground lies, and attempt to reach consensus about the most suitable candidate. The better approach is that of progressive elimination by which the weakest candidate is eliminated first, the second weakest next until the strongest candidate remains as the survivor. Although this may appear a more negative approach, it does begin with the most positive assumption, namely that all candidates are in the running until they are eliminated. The 'pick the winner' approach assumes that only one of the candidates could be the right choice. In addition the process of elimination does ensure that all aspects of the various candidates' abilities are examined and compared.

The chairperson should begin the review by reminding the panel of the purpose of the meeting by going over the job requirement details. When candidates have wide-ranging strengths and qualities it is all too easy to lose sight of the specific requirements which are being sought. Another important function of the chairperson is to require the panel members to provide evidence for the comments and evaluations they make. It is fatal to allow subjective evaluation and intuition to take over from a determination to come to terms with each candidate's abilities and potential.

This stage of the selection procedure should not be hurried. This does tend to happen when all the candidates are in a nearby room expectantly awaiting the outcome of the panel's deliberations. One of the purposes of the preliminary meeting held before the interviews was to agree a strategy for approaching the final selection. The chairperson plays a key role in keeping the discussion firmly fixed on the business in hand. He or she will need to summarize progress from time to time, and judge the right moment for making decisions. While unanimous agreement is the happiest outcome of selection deliberations, it is not always possible and the panel should be able to cope with a majority decision if it becomes necessary.

Once the decision has been made the selected candidate is contacted and offered the post. In the event of the offer being declined, the panel will have decided if another candidate is to be offered the post. If the offer is accepted then the unsuccessful candidates can be contacted immediately. There is no easy way of giving this information and a simple statement of fact, tinged with a note of regret, is usually the best approach. In the interests of good manners and communications this personal contact should be followed up with a personal letter which states who the successful candidate was, thanks candidates for applying and wishes them well in the future.

If a candidate asks for some feedback about interview ability, this should always be offered. It should note particularly the candidate's strong points, but also point out in general terms which professional attributes caused the panel the most concern.

Reference

POSTER, C. (1976) *School Decision-Making* London: Heinemann Educational

8   Staff Development

Commenting upon the findings of the HMI survey of primary education on its publication in September 1978, Norman Thomas, Chief
Inspector for Primary Schools, said: 'I have a plain message indeed. If
these specialist teachers are given status, time and the will to operate
we might make an advance in education.'[1] This statement summarizes
the essence of staff development, which is to create conditions in which
members of staff can work to the peak of their performance.

Schools have been rather slow to recognize how vital an aspect of
managing schools a concern for staff is. Teachers are the most costly
element of the educational enterprise and heads have not been
accustomed to consider them in investment terms. As pointed out in
the previous chapter, at current salary levels a teacher appointed to a
school for a period of five years represents an investment of about
£40,000. For a school of about 250 pupils the annual salary bill will be
in the region of £80,000. It is the head who carries the responsibility
for seeing that this money is wisely spent. Behind Norman Thomas's
emphatic words is a message which heads would do well to heed — the
responsibility for good teacher performance is a central aspect of
headship which the twin constraints of pupil:teacher ratio and capitation level do little to diminish.

Traditionally, staff development has been associated with in-service
training. For most teachers this has involved attendance at courses,
usually in their own time. The provision of in-service education and
training has been a shared responsibility between the DES, the LEAs,
the colleges and a few independent agencies. Despite heavy invest-
ments of money and attempts to improve coordination, there seems to

[1] Quoted in *Education*, vol.152, no.13, 29 September 1978.

be a general frustration within education that the key question of what professional development should really be about has not been adequately answered. There are a number of reasons for this. First, there has been little concerted effort to provide a systematic process of inservice training related to the needs of both the teachers and their schools. Course designers and organizers have tended to offer what they think will be popular among the local teaching force, working on the basis that a course needs to be well attended to be viable. Second, courses are offered to teachers whose individual experiences may be very different and whose needs may vary considerably. Third, a great deal of in-service training continues to use the very didactic methods that many courses have attempted to discourage teachers themselves from using. Fourth, there has developed an assumption that in-service training is a series of largely unconnected events.

The current circumstances of education make it even more important to develop a new paradigm of in-service education. In order to solve the staffing problems created by falling numbers on roll, most LEAs have been forced to introduce new regulations. Redeployment has been one means of solving the problem. While considerable time and energy is expended on the process of redeployment, perhaps not enough attention has been given to the professional development needs of those teachers who are redeployed. Far too often redeployment is regarded as a threat, when in reality it could be presented as an opportunity.

A further implication of falling rolls is a decrease in the number of opportunities for promotion. There is likely to be an increase in the number of amalgamations of separate infant and junior schools, and also the closure of the very smallest schools. Headships and deputy headships will become gradually more scarce, since the reduction in teacher numbers will not affect those most eligible for these senior posts. A readjustment of the Burnham scales could go some way to create a more satisfactory promotion structure within schools, but in the end it will fall to the schools themselves, and the heads in particular, to deal with the professional frustrations that may result from reduced job mobility.

No longer is it sufficient to regard the professional development of teachers as something which takes place only outside the school. The recent focus on school-based in-service training has perhaps more to do with financial restrictions than with a genuine desire to see the school as the main source of each teacher's professional development. However, positive change usually results when problems have a variety of causes. A general sense of dissatisfaction was referred to in the booklet *Making INSET Work* (DES 1978a). One paragraph in particular is relevant to the discussion here:

> INSET is a voluntary professional activity which depends for its success upon the goodwill of teachers. It is therefore vital that it should be relevant to staff

needs and of high quality. Too often in the past it has been thought of only in terms of individual teachers attending courses which are designed and provided by outside agencies. This discussion paper, while recognizing the extremely valuable contribution made by such courses, sets them in the context of a wider approach in which teachers and schools plan their own INSET programmes in the light of needs which they have identified.

The document was an attempt to create a new framework for professional development and suggested the following systematic approach:

1 identify the main needs
2 decide on and implement the general programme
3 evaluate the effectiveness of this general programme
4 follow up the ideas gained.

This attempts to place the emphasis on process, giving high priority to needs identification, programme evaluation and follow up, all aspects of in-service training which have traditionally had less than their fair share of attention. In their survey *Primary Education in England* (DES 1978b) HMI have a section entitled Staff Development, which draws attention to the need for an adequate provision of in-service training. The report not only emphasizes the fact that teachers need a continuous supporting pattern of training, but identifies two distinct functions for it:

> The first is to arrange for positive staff development based on the strengths of individuals. This should lead to extending the influence of experienced and able teachers. The second is to raise the expectations which teachers have of children and, in doing so, to achieve a clearer definition of the curriculum.

This quotation nicely emphasizes a point made very early in the book about the two main aspects of leadership – a concern for the tasks of the school, and a concern for the people who have to carry them out.

So, from a traditional concept of staff development as a series of events designed to provide opportunities for teachers to gain new ideas and acquire new skills, we are moving towards the idea of a process through which teachers can develop their professional competence and in so doing benefit themselves and the educational enterprise with which they are associated.

A framework for staff development

We can now define staff development as the process through which the professional competence of teachers is extended and their professional needs satisfied. It is concerned with individual aspirations and advancement, as well as with the collective development of the staff as a working team. Fig. 8.1 (p. 122) attempts to set the process in a

Development process over time	Professional categories	Competence factors
Identify needs	Teaching	Knowledge Skills Qualities
	Planning	Knowledge Skills Qualities
Create and implement programmes	Creating	Knowledge Skills Qualities
	Communicating	Knowledge Skills Qualities
Evaluate	Controlling	Knowledge Skills Qualities
	Motivating	Knowledge Skills Qualities
Follow up	Organizing	Knowledge Skills Qualities

Figure 8.1   Framework for staff development

framework. The professional categories are an attempt to isolate for consideration the separate activities with which teachers are most concerned. Clearly, the teaching category can be broken down into a whole range of constituent elements and this is an exercise the head will need to undertake with staff. The other categories are the six management functions already referred to in earlier chapters. They exist both within teaching activities, but also in addition to them, particularly if scale-post responsibility is involved.

The competence factors provide us with the means of considering

the three main elements which in combination determine performance. Briefly these can be defined as follows:

knowledge: knowing what needs to be done and how
skills: being able to do it
qualities: being aware of what is happening when you do it

It is the third factor which sadly has been missing from programmes of
initial and in-service training. In order to make the very best use of
knowledge and skills it is necessary to have a conscious awareness of the
effect of your endeavours upon those with whom you work, whether
they are children or colleagues, and to be sensitive to the subtle differences and variations in personality and character that exist within the
working group. It is the failure to take account of such personal
interaction factors that can produce the sorts of organizational stress
that result in low morale and poor professional performance.

The development process over time has two purposes. First, it
indicates that sequence of events to be pursued, either by individual
teachers alone or by the staff as a whole, and second, reinforces the
point that professional development is not a series of unrelated events
but a long-term process.

The role of the head

The staff of a school which lacks good leadership is unlikely to be
highly motivated. One of the indicators of good leadership is an
enthusiastic and committed staff working to high standards. The head
has to be skilful at maintaining this enthusiasm and ensuring that the
work the teachers do is satisfying and rewarding. But, there is a great
deal more to staff development than simply creating happy working
conditions. The lives of children and their learning prospects are at
stake and it does not follow that a happy staff is an effective one. The
head's overriding concern should be to provide the best possible
education for the pupils, and since this depends upon the teachers, it
is with their knowledge, skills and qualities that the head is most
concerned.

Staff development is a continuous exercise involving every working
member of the school. Staff development for caretakers and clerical
assistants is just as necessary as it is for teachers.

Many a head, following the taking stock exercise shortly after
appointment, has had cause to sit back and ponder on how to go about
changing the way teachers approach their professional work. There
are many approaches to this sometimes formidable task, ranging from
the blunt and blatant, to the subtle and ingenious. The strategy
recommended in this chapter is one that depends for its success upon
the existence of a climate of honesty and mutual trust between all
members of the teaching team.

Essentially, the head's task can be expressed in terms of four specific aims:

1 to know each teacher
2 to estimate potential
3 to assess achievement
4 to bridge the gap.

In some teachers the gap between their potential and their achievement is considerable, a factor which on occasions can cause heads to settle for less than they should. Before any of the formal elements of the staff development exercise are introduced, it is necessary to build the sort of working atmosphere in which professional growth can be encouraged. This depends in some measure on the following conditions being achieved:

1 A thorough knowledge and understanding by every member of staff of the philosophy, policies and procedures of the school.
2 An ability and willingness on the part of every member of staff to describe, explain and discuss their own approach to their work.
3 A thorough knowledge and understanding by every member of staff of each other's role within the school.
4 An ability for individual expertise to become known and shared.
5 The opportunity to meet and discuss common areas of concern.
6 An appreciation and acceptance that change is necessary if the school is to respond to new needs.
.7 An acceptance that the success of the school, in terms of the quality of education it achieves, is a shared responsibility.
8 A strong decision-making body.
9 Corporate leadership.
10 Excellent communications.

It is important at this stage to distinguish between the informal and formal system of staff development. Both are necessary if success is to be achieved, but the formal aspects should only be introduced when the informal system has succeeded in establishing the sorts of conditions outlined above. Some element of staff development will be present in most of the day-to-day activities which the head undertakes through work with individual teachers, and with the staff as a whole. The formal system becomes established when there is a general desire within the staff for a specific policy and procedure. In some schools the head may feel that informal proceedings will be necessary for some time, while in others it may be possible to introduce a specific policy quite early in an administration.

The informal system in action

As an example of the informal system in operation, I will describe the series of events in one particular school where a new head had just been appointed.

The school was an inner city primary with 285 children on roll. The new head took up her appointment in January, after six years as head of a suburban infant school. The staffing was organized as follows:

Head:
Deputy: Staff duty rotas/Boys' discipline
Scale 3:   Head of infants/Girls' welfare
Scale 2:   Boys' games
Scale 2:   Needlework
Scale 2:   Library
Scale 2:   Pottery/Display
Scale 2:   Environmental Studies
Scale 1:   Probationary teacher
Scale 1:   "   "

Staff morale was not high when the head took over the school. The pressures of inner city life were wearing and, despite many attempts, no member of staff had been promoted out of the school for over five years. Two members of staff had retired at the end of the previous summer term and the probationers who replaced them were the first new members of staff for four years.

During her first term the new head made a number of organizational changes and spent a great deal of her time around the school and in the classrooms. She had told the staff that her first task was to get to know them, the children and something of the life of the school, and that if she felt major changes were necessary she would consult them. A basic and consistent good humour, coupled with her energy and enthusiasm, did result in improved relationships in the staffroom, and in a more positive and relaxed atmosphere in the school generally.

At the end of the spring term, and as the result of a comprehensive taking stock exercise, the head prepared a detailed report for her governing body. It it she outlined a number of areas where she felt improvements were needed. These she declared were contingent upon the achievement of a new spirit of willingness and cooperation from her colleagues and that the main impetus of her policy would be directed towards this end.

During the summer term the head initiated two main types of activity:

1 *Information exchange.* This involved using the last twenty minutes of the weekly staff meeting to announce and discuss items which had arisen since the last meeting. Each member of staff in turn was invited to make a contribution.

2   *Informal discussion.* This involved regular discussions between the
    head and each individual member of staff. Invariably they took .
    place in the classroom at the end of each day. The head attempted
    to see each member of staff at least once each week on this basis, in
    addition to their more casual conversations in the staffroom.

Towards the end of the summer term a number of developments were
worthy of note. The information exchange had developed from a
rather abrupt self-conscious affair into a dynamic interchange of
ideas. Success was assisted by the fact that the two probationary
teachers, despite having already spent two terms in the school, knew
little of the philosophy of the school or of the schemes of work which
existed. The head had encouraged the two probationers to use the
information exchange to seek answers to their questions. This they did
and the staff welcomed the opportunity to talk about the school in a
way they had not been encouraged to before. A number of the issues
raised required special meetings and these were held in addition to the
weekly staff meeting after school, usually in a lunch-time·and often
involving a sub-group of staff members.
    Most of the staff had welcomed the interest of the head in their
classrooms and by building positive and encouraging relationships
with her colleagues she began to attract a measure of loyalty and
support.
    Another strategy the head had employed was to devolve a good deal
of the routine decision-making to key members of staff. The deputy
head found himself having to make a vastly increased range of
decisions, and after the initial shock, began to enjoy the increased
status that his enlarged role in the school created. The whole staff was
involved as never before in the exercise to plan the allocation of
children and teachers to classes for the next academic year.
    Towards the end of the summer term the head felt confident that an
improved morale among the staff and a strong measure of support for
what she already had done would justify the launching of her first
major proposal for change. It had become clear to her, both through
observation of the school at work and with her discussions with staff,
that a major curriculum review of the school was necessary. The
schemes of work that did exist were scrappy and out of date, school
resources and equipment were in a bad state and there was little
attention to continuity and progression from one year to another. Her
main realization, however, was that if any major advance in
curriculum development was to be made possible it would have to be
achieved with the active cooperation of the staff. She decided to build
on the already improving morale by giving it a greater sense of direction. This would involve a review of the scale-post structure, so that by
the end of the next academic year the staff themselves with their new
areas of responsibility would be instrumental in pressing for change.

The opportunity to present the proposal to the staff arose out of a casual conversation in the staffroom. Suggestions had been made for a staff social function at the end of term. These ranged from hiring a coach for an outing for the staff and their families to an evening meal at a local hotel. The staff had already decided to come into school during the holiday for a staff meeting, so after further deliberation a novel compromise was agreed to. A conference room at a local hotel was to be booked for a day. The staff would meet there and be joined by partners and friends for a buffet supper in the evening.

The head undertook considerable and detailed planning for this conference. She visited the hotel to ensure that circumstances were conducive to a comfortable and relaxed atmosphere and that there was adequate provision for the whole staff to convene, as well as for individual and small group work. The last two staff meetings of the term were devoted to conference planning and the following agenda was agreed to:

10.00	Coffee
10.30	Presentation and discussion of paper *Towards New Responsibilities*.
11.30	Coffee
11.45	Individual and small group work
12.30	Lunch
1.45	Progress report
2.30	Individual and small group work
3.15	Tea
3.30	Information exchange

In her paper the head attempted to emphasize how important to the quality of education within the school was the role of the scale-post holder. She pointed out why she felt the present structure was not working to full advantage and provided a framework upon which discussion could build. Her final point was that responsibility roles had to change and develop as the needs of the school changed, and that posts would need to be reviewed annually if they were to continue to be effective. A copy of this paper together with the printed agenda for the conference was posted to each member of staff a week before the conference date.

The day arrived and the proceedings began. In the first session the head introduced her paper. During the discussion it became very clear that many of the staff were frustrated in their specialist roles. Some of the contributing factors to this frustration raised during the discussion were:

lack of job descriptions
lack of time to undertake tasks
poor communications
lack of real authority and responsibility

inadequate resources
lack of overall school policy
not knowing previous head's expectations
not knowing other colleagues' responsibilities
failures to gain promotion
scale-post activities not acknowledged or appreciated.

There was general agreement that any new system would have to make very clear the nature, range and extent of scale-post duties. There was also genuine concern that the organization of primary schools made it very difficult to combine satisfactorily general class teaching duties with scale-post responsibilities. The point was made very strongly by one of the teachers that scale-post work must be for the mutual support and benefit of the more general class teaching enterprise.

After coffee the staff divided into three small groups, the head circulating between each. The groups were asked to consider the three models of scale-post responsibility – curriculum, organization and leadership, and to generate specific ideas for posts of responsibility within each of the categories. The suggestions were recorded on cards.

After lunch the whole staff convened to consider the various suggestions. As each model was discussed the cards were arranged in piles of similar suggestions. This session, and the one immediately before lunch, suffered because of pressure of time. Instead of concentrating their efforts on getting their ideas down on the cards, too much time was spent in examining and arguing about the different suggestions. (The technique of brainstorming outlined in Chapter 4 would have helped to overcome this.) However, a good collection of suggestions was eventually assembled. The school secretary who had joined the staff for lunch took all the cards back to school, typed them up and photocopied them for distribution during the final session. The lists were as follows:

Curriculum Posts
Basic Studies (remedial work)
Mathematics
Language Development
Physical Education
Aesthetic Development
Creative Arts
Humanities
Environmental Studies
Project Work
Science
Organization Posts
Resources and resource centre
Stock control

Timetabling
School trips and journeys
Library
School Museums Service
PTA
Liaison and transfer
Leadership Posts
Year coordinators
Curriculum Development
Head of Infants
Head of Juniors

During the session immediately before tea each member of staff was asked to work out their own suggested timetable of events for the next academic year, fitting in the following key stages:

1   designation of new posts
2   circulation of new role definitions
3   circulation of curriculum development plan discussion document.

After working out individual timetables the staff convened into their small groups and attempted to negotiate an agreed proposal.

During the final session, the by now familiar information exchange, the three timetables proposals were negotiated into an agreed plan and the progress and achievements of the day were reviewed. The timetable agreed to was:

By Autumn half term	Agreement on new scale-post structure and designation of new posts
By end of Autumn term	Role definitions agreed and circulated.
By Spring half term	Draft development plans in each area of responsibility circulated
By end of Spring term	Terms of reference for curriculum review agreed
By end of Summer term	Plans and timetable for curriculum review agreed

The lists of suggested scale posts was circulated and the progress and achievements of the day reviewed. Finally each participant was in turn invited to declare their reactions to the conference and to share with colleagues the experiences they had valued most during the day. The school secretary sat in on this session and took a shorthand report of this discussion, an edited edition of which was duplicated for the future benefit of the staff. A copy of this, and the other documents resulting from the day, were sent to the LEA whose in-service fund had paid for the hiring of the conference room. (Staff paid for their own meal and refreshment expenses.)

Among individual reactions to the conference were:

'Too much to do in too little time.'

'Most refreshing and stimulating, a personal tonic.'

'How different the problems are when you take them out of school.'

'How incredible to have a staff meeting without any interruptions.'

'There is a danger that you could become divorced from reality and develop only theoretical solutions.'

'If we did this more regularly we could solve almost anything.'

'Let's reorganize the staffroom.'

Beneath a certain euphoria, perhaps due to the novelty of the occasion, some of the generic problems of school decision-making can be discerned: lack of time; unsuitable venues for meetings; lack of clear direction to meetings.

From the head's point of view the conference achieved far more than she had dared hope. Not only had she got her staff sitting down together with a new spirit of commitment and enthusiasm, but they had succeeded in generating positive suggestions for future development and in agreeing the form and sequence these would take during the next academic year. Her pleasure in achieving this excellent start was sobered only by the realization that future success would depend very much upon her skills in management and leadership.

Before leaving this example there are two further points to be made. First, it later transpired that one of the key aspects of the day conference was the production of papers documenting the proceedings of the various sessions. There were a number of occasions during ensuing terms when these papers were necessary to indicate the progress that was being made, to inject new motivation when progress was slow, and to remind staff of agreements already made. Documentation is essential to good decision-making, and it is all too easy to forget the circumstances in which earlier decisions were made and to lose the vital threads of development and direction. The second point refers to the two probationary teachers. How did they relate to the exercise which was essentially concerned with Scale 2 and 3 responsibilities? Both teachers had discussed this issue with the head, both during earlier informal discussions and later when the final arrangements for the conference were being made. Both had responded eagerly to the development plans and offered to take a share of extra responsibility despite the fact that this could not, at this stage, be rewarded by extra payment.

The formal system

The formal system of staff development differs from the informal in that the policy itself, and the procedures for implementing it, are the subject of staff discussion and agreement. The system needs careful structure if all the partners in the exercise are to derive the full benefits.

To facilitate planning for staff development the four aims described above can be related to the framework outlined in Fig. 8.1 (p. 122). This now gives us a clear relationship between the aims and the process over time:

AIMS   PROCESS
To know each teacher
To estimate potential   Indentify needs
To assess performance

                                    Create and implement programme
To bridge the gap   Evaluate programme
                                    Follow up

The framework provides the outline for a detailed professional profile of each member of staff. Some aspects of this profile will have been completed during the taking stock exercise early in headship, when the following details will have been ascertained:

1   qualifications and training
2   background and experience
3   current teaching role
4   current scale-post responsibility
5   variety of experience within the school
6   in-service record
7   professional reading and study
8   enthusiasms, interest and expertise
9   career aspirations

As working relationships develop between the head and staff, further knowledge and understanding will be gained, and this can provide a basis for estimating potential and assessing results. The framework outlines the headings under which a series of checklists can be prepared. For example:

Professional category   Teaching
Competence factor   Knowledge
                          1   of child development
                          2   of learning styles
                          3   of curriculum design
                          4   of teaching strategies
                          5   of evaluation procedures
                          Skills
                          1   in teaching
                          2   in relationships with children
                          3   in assessing children's attitudes
                          4   in matching work to ability

5   in evaluating progress
Qualities
1   motivating children
2   awareness of individual needs
3   fostering and maintaining learning

To achieve a complete picture of a teacher's professional competence, checklists for the six management functions will also be necessary.

Most heads, when preparing a confidential report on a colleague seeking promotion, will make reference to

1   teaching competence
2   quality of relationships
3   personal qualities as a staff member
4   scale-post responsibilities
5   professional attitudes
6   estimate of potential for the post under consideration.

These sorts of comments involve a range of judgments which in the case of references and confidential reports are the head's alone. A vital element of positive staff development is the process of staff evaluation from as wide a base as possible. In making recommendations to a fellow head it is important to present as comprehensive and accurate a profile of the member of staff seeking the post as possible. Teachers need to appreciate the necessity for evaluation, and they are more likely to do so if they are fully involved in the process. A formal policy for staff development facilitates this. The two main elements of the system are: the personal file and the appraisal interview.

The personal file

This will need to contain:

1   role definition
2   year plans
3   term plans
4   action programmes
5   professional development programmes
6   self evaluation reports
7   appraisal interview reports
8   copies of references and confidential reports
9   notes on promotion interviews and feedback from advisers
10 scale-post reports to governors
11 papers prepared for staff discussion
12 relevant correspondence
13 miscellaneous notes by the teacher
14 miscellaneous notes by the head.

Such a file is both a document of achievement and a declaration of intent, and provides valuable evidence of professional development. It is a confidential file to which only the teacher concerned and the head should have access. For the teacher it will be a record of professional progress in which previous plans are related to the consequent results. For the head it is the means by which to create a positive professional dialogue with colleagues, assist in their development, and in so doing serve the best educational interests of the school.

The appraisal interview

The other vital element at the heart of good staff development is the regular interview between the head and each member of staff. Ideally this should take place every term and anything less than once a year is hardly staff development. The main purpose is to review progress since the previous interview. On most occasions this will involve:

1 reviewing outcomes of previous plans
2 considering future plans
3 resolving problems
4 reinforcing progress.

If these interviews are to be successful the head has to realize that they are not occasions on which to influence colleagues. The emphasis should be on helping members of staff to consider their own positions, define their own problems and discover their own practical solutions. The interview should be conducted on equal terms in an open and honest way. The head needs to be both objective yet encouraging, and use skilful questioning to help a colleague to get to the heart of the issues under discussion.

A termly meeting will include a consideration of the term plan and its attendant action programme. In reviewing past objectives it is important to remember that evaluation should be based on results and not intentions. Failure to achieve objectives is as likely to be the result of over enthusiasm as of inadequate performance. The head has to help each colleague to set realistic targets so that the review does not reveal too wide a gap between outcomes and intentions.

It is during the appraisal interview that performance is evaluated. One of the features of a staff development system that is working well is the staffs' willingness to consider the issue of assessing performance, and it is often the case that teachers will be more openly critical of themselves than the head would ever dare be. To get the full benefits from this process some scheme for positive self assessment is required. A series of self assessment checklists related to the framework for staff development can prove helpful here. Carefully thought-out questions can often do more to help a teacher to focus on the important details of performance than can the comments of an observer.

The appraisal interview will also include some consideration of the professional development programme. For some teachers this might incorporate activities that will take a year to complete. Occasionally the programme will cover an even longer period if, for example, a two-year part-time diploma course is being undertaken. Perhaps for most teachers the best approach is to plan a programme for the year and review its progress each term. Once individual needs have been identified the means of satisfying them have to be found. These might include:

1   direct help from a colleague within the school
2   a visit or visits to other schools
3   help from advisory colleagues
4   attendance at a specific course or series of courses
5   professional reading and study
6   teaching a different age-range
7   trying a new form of class organization
8   a change of scale-post responsibility
9   exchanging with a teacher in another school

For some teachers a single event might suffice, but for most the programme will consist of a variety of activities. Thought has to be given to the sequence of events and also to how they are spread within the time available. It will be helpful if, in addition to some general aims for the programme, some specific objectives are established, for this is the key to sound evaluation.

When a programme has been completed and the evaluation undertaken the question of follow-up arises. If new skills have been acquired how will they now be employed, and how might future teaching plans attempt to incorporate them? Will there be opportunities for newly-acquired expertise to be made available to the staff, and in which particular ways will the children benefit?

Whole-staff development

It sometimes happens that the process of curriculum change makes it necessary for the whole staff to acquire new knowledge and skills. In this situation perhaps the best approach is to seek the help of the advisory service in setting up a school-based in-service programme. Careful planning is essential. For example, if visiting speakers are to be used they should be asked to supply a list of preparatory considerations before the visit and leave some points for discussion after it. Some parts of the programme should be designed to provide opportunities for the staff to work in small groups, and there should be elements for individual consideration. By way of illustration I use the example of a school which was to move out of its old decaying premises into a new open-plan building. The head, who had previous experience of team-teaching in an open-plan school, was aware that quite fundamental changes in professional attitudes would be necessary if the transition from one approach to education to another was to be successful.

Before considering the curriculum and organization the head arranged for the architect to come to school on two occasions to talk with the staff about the design of the new school. He also persuaded the architect to provide a copy of the plans for each member of staff. In the first meeting the architect talked about the brief she had been given by the Education Department and shared with the staff the ideas that were currently influencing the design of schools.

In the two weeks between her visits the staff met on a number of occasions to look at the plans and talk about the new school. It was clear that the staff were finding it difficult to translate the architect's plans into a visual picture of what the school would eventually look like inside, and that this would inhibit any detailed planning they would have to undertake. Before her next visit the head telephoned the architect and pointed out this difficulty, also mentioning some of the other points raised in the staff discussions. On her next visit the meeting was held in one of the infant classrooms. With the aid of all the wooden bricks and blocks the staff could muster the architect built a model that enabled the staff to gain a much clearer picture of what their new school was to be like. She also pointed out that the design incorporated elements already tried out in three other schools in the authority and suggested that the staff might like to visit these.

The visits were duly arranged and the heads and teachers of the visited schools made themselves available to explain and discuss how they had approached the task of changing from one style of learning organization to another. Following these visits the head next sought the help of the adviser for primary education, and together they began to plan a school-based in-service programme for the eighteen months leading up to the move to the new building. After the draft plan was discussed with the staff, and their views incorporated, the final plan was agreed to. The two-year programme worked out as follows:

Autumn Term
1   First visit of architect
2   Staff discussion
3   Staff discussion
4   Second visit of architect
Spring Term
1   Visit to school A
2   Visit to school B
3   Visit to school C
4   Staff discussion
5   Staff discussion

Summer Term

1 ⎫
2 ⎬ Planning meetings − head and adviser
3 ⎭

4 ⎫ Draft programme circulated and discussed
5 ⎪ Staff working in small groups to
6 ⎬ (a) identify hopes for the new school
7 ⎪ (b) discuss worries and concerns about the move
8 ⎭ (c) identify specific needs

Autumn Term

1 ⎫ Whole staff discussion of head's paper. 'Some approaches to
2 ⎭ vertical-grouping and team-teaching'
3   Visit to School B to see team-teaching in operation

4 ⎫
5 ⎬ Each teacher to exchange with a colleague from School B to
6 ⎭ experience team-teaching in action

7 ⎫ Whole staff discussion
8 ⎭

Spring Term

1 ⎫ Final plans outlined for organization of each teaching unit and
2 ⎭ definition of new roles and responsibilities

3 ⎫
4 ⎪
5 ⎬ Curriculum review meetings
6 ⎪
7 ⎭

Summer Term

1 ⎫ Preparation of:
2 ⎪ (a) Year plan for each teaching unit − an outline of the year's
3 ⎪   work agreed between two teachers
4 ⎬ (b) Term plan − termly objectives for each individual teacher
5 ⎪ (c) Action programmes − to be arranged in weekly team
6 ⎪   meetings
7 ⎪ (d) Coordination plans − the four scale-post holders to prepare
8 ⎭   plans for coordination and support in their specialist areas of
       responsibility

Few whole-staff programmes will be concerned with developments on this scale and most are best conceived in months rather than years. A well-designed programme will focus on the whole-staff element, but will also allow for individual and group variation within it. As in any planning activity it is essential to establish clear aims and objectives for the programme so that a sense of direction is maintained.

While this chapter has been concerned to identify some of the elements of a positive staff development policy, it must be remembered that the process of professional development is reflected in most of the activities of the school. It is present in the way decisions are arrived at, in the way responsibility is shared, and in the way the curriculum is interpreted and implemented. Staff development is the single most important activity the head is concerned with. Not only do staff have the right to professional support from their head, but the very success of the educational enterprise depends upon it.

References

DES (1978a) *Making INSET Work* London: HMSO
DES (1978b) *Primary Education in England: A Survey by HM Inspectors of Schools* London: HMSO

9 Evaluation and Accountability

An earlier chapter of this book placed evaluation as the final stage of the decision-making process. It is important to stress at the outset of this chapter the cyclic nature of that process:

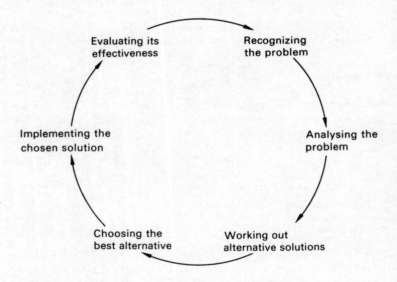

Figure 9.1   The decision-making process

Bad management can result from the misconception that evaluation is simply the final stage of a process. It needs to be seen as that part of the process which links again with future developments, making continuity and progression possible. Only if future actions are informed by the experience of previous ones will steady progress be made.

In recent years there has been an increasing demand for accountability. This has created the need for a more systematic approach to the process of evaluating education at all its various levels. The Assessment of Performance Unit was established by the Department of Education and Science to provide a national picture of pupil performance in certain agreed aspects of the curriculum. HMI have attempted a comprehensive analysis of the educational process in their surveys of first, primary, middle and secondary schools. Research projects too help to provide answers to questions about how effective our education system is. The ORACLE project – a most important large-scale observational study of primary schools – has now been carried out and the reports of the project raise questions of considerable significance for heads and teachers in primary schools (Galton *et al.* 1980; Galton and Simon 1980).

The main purpose of this chapter is to emphasize how necessary it is for each school to be actively involved in evaluating its own performance. The argument is well summarized by Marten Shipman in his practical guide *In-school Evaluation* (Shipman 1979):

> Evaluation is a basic management tool in all organizations. Throughout this book the search is for information on performance that will help in decision-making. This information, produced by evaluation, does not determine the decisions. But the judgments that lead to decisions are informed by the evaluation.

Although written with the secondary school in mind this book has a great deal that will be of interest and help to those heads and teachers in primary schools who are concerned to find effective ways of evaluating their schools.

The need for a more systematic approach to evaluation was noted in *Education in Schools: A Consultative Document* (DES 1977):

> 3.3 Growing recognition of the need for schools to demonstrate their accountability to the society which they serve requires a coherent and soundly-based means of assessment for the educational system as a whole, for schools and for individual pupils.
> 3.7 . . . Such assessment will take account of examination and test results, but will also depend heavily on a detailed knowledge of the circumstances of the schools by the authorities' officers, their inspectors and advisers, and such self assessment as may be undertaken by the schools. . . .

Further emphasis to this was given in the final paragraph of *A View of the Curriculum* (DES 1980):

> In the end, whatever is decided nationally must leave much for individual local education authorities and schools to determine as they interpret the

national agreement to take account of the nature of individual schools and individual pupils. It must take account of children's capacity to learn at any given stage of their maturity and identify what is intrinsically worth learning and best acquired through schooling. It must, too, allow for future modification in response to new needs in the world outside schools. Decisions cannot sensibly be taken once and for all. The effort involved will be justified if it leads to developing more fully the potential of all children.

An element of evaluation is present in a great deal of the work that a head does. Of the six management functions outlined earlier in the book, it is that of controlling with which we are most concerned here. This function is about keeping the school working towards its planned intentions. For the head this involves comparing outcomes with plans and taking corrective action where necessary. But it is the precise means of doing this which can pose difficulties. Within the cognitive domain of the curriculum the measurement of pupil performance is not difficult to arrange, and many schools carry out some form of testing in reading, comprehension and mathematics. Within the affective domain, the problem of assessment is more difficult. Many teachers perhaps subscribe to the view that only standardized tests can be objective, and that teacher-designed and teacher-controlled evaluation is subjective and therefore somehow unreliable.

Since the schools in our education system are given considerable freedom to interpret and develop for themselves a curriculum suited to the needs of their individual pupils, it is necessary that they respond in a professional way by developing methods of evaluation designed to measure how far their particular curriculum is achieving its intentions. The key to success in this process lies in the relationship between planning and evaluation. If the curriculum of a school is expressed in a handful of loosely defined aims and no more, then evaluation becomes extremely difficult. If, however, specific objectives are derived in the manner described in Chapter 5, then the process can become much easier to handle. Much will depend upon how well objectives are constructed and how precisely they are phrased. They will need to distinguish between knowledge, skills and qualities and have regard for the age of the pupil and his stage of development.

Far too often evaluation is regarded in a rather negative way as 'checking up'. It is essential to develop positive attitudes towards it so that it is seen as a systematic process designed to make the school a more effective place for its learners. This is more likely to be successful if curriculum aims and objectives are constantly in the minds of the head and staff, and are a ready source of discussion. It is at the curriculum planning stage that evaluation checklists can be prepared. These are closely related to objectives and are best written in the form of questions to the teacher. Using the example of the world studies course described in Chapter 5, the checklist could well begin as follows:

1 (i) a
   (i) How well is the pupil able to *describe* the culture to which he belongs?
   (ii) How well is the pupil able to *describe* his own place in society?

1 (i) b
   (i) How well is the pupil able to *explain* how his own society works?
   (ii) How well is the pupil able to *explain* why aspects of his own society and culture are as they are?

Such questions as these involve judgments by the teacher about the level of performance of the pupil. Evaluation of this sort needs to be applied during the programme of work, on its completion and at future dates, particularly if other courses have the same or similar objectives. A useful device to assist this process is a pupil evaluation sheet (see Fig. 9.2). The amount of shading in the squares will relate to a demostrated level of competence in terms of knowledge gained, skill developed or quality acquired. A very helpful source book for this technique is *Match and Mismatch* by Wynne Harlen (1977). This type of evaluation provides for the teacher information of two sorts. First, it indicates the level of individual pupil achievement; second, it

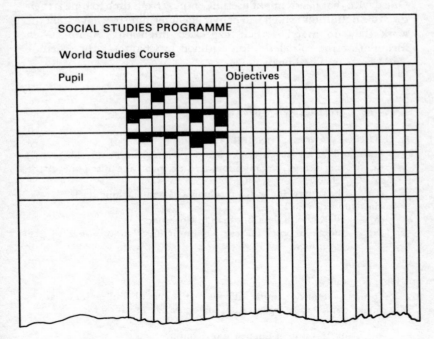

Figure 9.2   Pupil evaluation sheet

reflects how successfully pupils as a whole have achieved the intentions of specific learning experiences. It should also help to determine how well work has been matched to the varying abilities of the pupils involved.

The publication by the DES of the National Primary Survey in 1978 presented heads with a unique opportunity to undertake a process of evaluation which would relate the work of their own schools to the findings expressed in the report. As well as the findings of the survey, which pose questions for all primary schools, there are the schedules already referred to in Chapter 5. These list a wide range of curriculum factors which HMI used as the basis of their observations in the schools surveyed. A most useful evaluation schedule for a primary school can be produced simply by rephrasing the schedule statements into question form. By seeking answers to these questions the head and staff would obtain a comprehensive insight into the work of their school. The survey is evidence that evaluation by direct observation is both objective and reliable.

So far we have given brief consideration to curriculum evaluation. What we are more concerned with in this book is the process of organizational evaluation which the head will need to apply to the school as a whole. Here the head is concerned not only to evaluate the learning programmes but also his or her own management strategies. One device that heads might usefully employ from time to time is their own role definition, which will help them determine to what extent the work they do matches their expressed intentions. Again, when formulating the role definition outlined in Chapter 1 the schedule could be as outlined below.

Role evaluation schedule

AUTHORITY AND RESPONSIBILITY
1 How familiar are the governors with my strategies for controlling:
   (a)   the internal organization, management and discipline of the school?
   (b)   the supervision of the teaching and non-teaching staff?
2 How and when do I:
   (a)   consult with the Chairman of Governors?
   (b)   submit reports on curriculum matters to meetings of the governors?

ORGANIZATION
1 To what extent do I work with the staff to create and maintain an efficient and happy organization, particularly in relation to:
   (a)   staffing
   (b)   distribution of finance and resources
   (c)   supervision of pupils?

2 How do I go about creating and maintaining a decision-making structure which provides facilities for participation by the staff?
3 How efficient is my system of commuication?

PEOPLE
1 How is my teaching programme organized? How many of the children in the school do I work with regularly?
2 How often do I have personal contacts with each member of the teaching and non-teaching staff?
3 How do I help, support and advise each member of staff to pursue their duties and develop their careers?
4 How do I make myself available to:
   (a) children
   (b) teachers
   (c) non-teaching staff
   (d) governors
   (e) parents
   (f) LEA officials
   (g) HMI
   (h) visitors?

Further self evaluation can be undertaken by relating the six management functions to each action programme as it is completed. A most useful and revealing exercise for heads is to note down during one week the details of all the work they undertake. This is a technique recommended by Peter Drucker in *The Effective Executive* (1967). As he says:

> For all these reasons, the demands of the organization, the demands of people, the time demands of change and innovation, it will become increasingly important for executives to be able to manage their time. But one cannot even think of managing one's time unless one first knows where it goes.

One of the great difficulites of headship is separating the important from the merely urgent. From the week's work the head can see what proportion of time was given to:

1 planning ⎤
2 creating
3 communicating
4 controlling
5 motivating   Planned activities
6 organizing
7 teaching
8 routine administration ⎦

9 unplanned activities

The proportion of planned to unplanned activities will reveal much about the head's management competence, and a more detailed analysis of time allocated to the six management functions could indicate areas which are being neglected. No head should set out with the intention of eradicating the urgent and unplanned activities, for it is these aspects of headship which lift it out of the realms of the routine and predictable. But too much time on the unplanned will distract the head from central purposes. In an attempt to bring time under control Drucker recommends the following:

> One has to find the non-productive, time-wasting activities and get rid of them if one possibly can. This requires asking oneself a number of diagnostic questions.

> First one tries to identify and eliminate the things that need not be done at all, the things that are purely waste of time without any results whatever. To find these time-wastes, one asks of *all* activities in the time records 'What would happen if this were not done at all?' And if the answer is, 'Nothing would happen' then obviously the conclusion is to stop doing it.'

The chapter from which these quotations are taken is called 'Know Thy Time' and is an excellent strategy for improving management efficiency.

Another set of questions can focus on the three modes of leadership:

> When working with my colleagues how often am I:
> (a) a colleague
> (b) a guide
> (c) a leader?

It would be possible to create evaluation schedules which consist of a series of headings for consideration, but there is something infinitely more challenging and demanding about a well-phrased question. An interesting example of this technique is *Keeping the School Under Review* (ILEA Inspectorate 1977). Produced by a group of head-teachers and staff inspectors in the Inner London Education Authority, this booklet sets out a method of self assessment for schools. As the Foreword explains:

> What this paper offers is not a blue print or questionnaire to be rigorously followed or answered in its entirety every year. It is presented as a basis for the development of a school's own form of self assessment, to be modified or extended to suit the intentions and interests of the individual school.

It is in the same vein that the following checklists are offered. They raise a series of questions related to the points made in each of the chapters. They are models for consideration rather than definitive examples of one form of the evaluation process and are intended to help heads in their self appraisal.

Evaluation checklists

1 Towards a role definition

Presciptions

How do the following affect my role:
(a) 1944 Education Act
(b) 1980 Education Act
(c) Health and Safety at Work Act 1974
(d) common law responsibilities
(e) Rules of Government
(f) LEA directives and regulations
(g) contract of employment?

Expectations

How is my role influenced by the expectations of:
(a) children
(b) parents
(c) governors
(d) the local education authority
(e) staff?

Situations

Which particular cirumstances of this school affect my role?

Predilections

What are my hopes and intentions for this school?

Defining the role

1 for whom am I responsible?
2 to whom am I responsible?
3 with whom am I responsible?
4 for what am I responsible?

Role definition

1 How was my role definition created?
2 Does it make reference to:
(a) authority and responsibility
(b) the curriculum
(c) the organization of the school
(d) people?

3   Does it take account of all the six management functions?
4   Who has copies of my role definition?
5   Do I use my role definition as a basis for planning my work?
6   How often do I review my role definition?
7   Do I use it as a means of evaluating my work?

2 Taking over

Before taking up the post

1   What are my aims in education?
2   What is my view of the curriculum?
3   What are my opinions of the various teaching styles?
4   What sort of learning environment do I favour?
5   What sort of social order will I want to encourage?

Preappointment visits

1   What are the purposes of these visits?
2   Who will I need to meet before taking up my appointment?
3   What knowledge of the school do I need to gain from these visits?

Prior to first day in post

1   How well do I know the catchment area?
2   How familiar am I with the school site and building?
3   Have I prepared my office so that it is
(a)   conducive to private conversation
(b)   welcoming to visitors
(c)   well organized for efficient work?
4   How do I intend that my office should be used?
5   How do I intend that children and staff should regard it?

The first day

1   What sort of impression do I intend to make?
2   What shall I do when I arrive?
3   How will I make contact with each member of staff?
4   What will be the theme of my first assembly?
5   What do I hope to have achieved by the end of the first day?

Taking stock

1   What information do I need about the school?
2   How can I obtain it?
3   How long do I intend to take over it?

Collecting information

1   In gathering the necessary information how can I best use:
(a)   personal observation

(b)   informal contacts
(c)   formal methods
     documents
     formal interviews
     questionnaires
     staff meetings?
2   How will the information be documented?
3   How will the data I have gathered be analysed?
4   Does my report identify what needs to be done?
5   How can I now order my priorities in relation to
(a)   my year plan
(b)   my term plan
(c)   my immediate action programme?

3 A question of style

1   What is my definition of leadership?
2   How much importance do I attach to the need to know and understand the people I work with?
3   What will be my strengths and weaknesses in this area of my work?
4   How do I see the relationship between a concern for the tasks of the school and a concern for the people who have to undertake them?
5   Are all my staff clear about
(a)   their own roles and those of their colleagues
(b)   the goals of the school
(c)   the procedures by which decisions are made
(d)   the procedures for evaluating the work of the school?
6   How can I best encourage the development of
(a)   the skills of the staff
(b)   the confidence they have in their abilities
(c)   their desire to initiate
(d)   their need to accept responsibility?
7   Is my work firmly based in the six functions of management?
(a)   planning
(b)   creating
(c)   communicating
(d)   controlling
(e)   motivating
(f)   organizing
8   Am I clear about the differences between
(a)   authority
(b)   power
(c)   responsibility
(d)   accountability?
9   In terms of my leadership style, how often am I
(a)   a colleague
(b)   a guide
(c)   a leader?

10   How much consideration and time do I give to developing my relationships
(a)   with each individual member of staff
(b)   with the staff as a whole?
11   Am I aware of their perceptions of me, and of the consequences that my behaviour has on them?
12   How honest and frank are my relationships with my colleagues?
13   Do I construct unnecessary barriers?
14   How do I see the communications network of my school?
15   How do I set about managing the variety of communications tasks?
16   How well do the official communications procedures of the school work?
17   How strong and active is the 'grapevine'?
18   To what extent do personal factors enhance or inhibit the communications system of the school?
19   Do I constantly and patiently seek answers to the following questions?
(a)   who ought to know what?
(b)   how do they get to know?
(c)   how do I know that they know?

4 Decision-making

1   In what areas of the curriculum can decisions be made without reference to me?
2   In which aspects of the school organization are important decisions made by a member of staff other than me?
3   Do I insist on being consulted over every important decision made in my school?

The decision-making process

1   Do I have a clearly structured process for decision-making?
2   How are issues for decision-making identified?
3   How are they analysed?
4   How are alternative solutions developed?
5   Are alternative solutions tested against the range of relevant criteria?
6   How is the choice from alternative solutions made?
7   How is the implementation planned?
8   Does the implementation plan identify tasks, associated roles and responsibilities and the dates for completion?
9   How will the outcomes of important decision-making be evaluated?

Participation

1   To what extent are the staff involved in the decision-making process?
2   Are they active at every stage of the process?
3   Do I encourage the development of decision-making skills in individuals, and in the staff as a whole?

4 How much decision-making is undertaken without my active involvement?

Meetings

1 For what purposes are staff meetings held?
2 How frequently are they held?
3 Is an agenda circulated before meetings?
4 Can any member of staff request an agenda item?
5 Are minutes taken and circulated?
6 Do I make a distinction between decision-making meetings and those held for routine administrative purposes?
7 What are my strengths and weaknesses in conducting meetings?
8 Am I helping to develop small-group skills in my colleagues?

5 Planning the curriculum

1 To what extent has the curriculum of my school been influenced by
(a) national curriculum traditions
(b) children
(c) teachers
(d) governors
(e) parents
(f) the LEA
(g) public expectations?
2 To what extent have the following specific factors influenced the curriculum of my school?
(a) the design of the building
(b) the history of the school
(c) finance
(d) resources
(e) the decision-making process
(f) transfer policies
(g) catchment area
3 To what extent does the curriculum reflect the hopes and aspirations of myself and my staff?

Establishing goals

1 Are the curriculum intentions for the school written down?
2 Are all members of staff familiar with them?
3 In planning or reviewing the curriculum do I take account of
(a) the need to gain agreement
(b) the importance of involving staff in the process of making curriculum decisions?

Determining methods

1 How are the following decisions made?
(a) who will teach what?

(b)   how will it be taught?
(c)   when will it be taught?
2   To what extent are issues of teaching style discussed and agreed upon?
3   Are all members of staff familiar with the teaching styles of their colleagues?
4   Are all staff familiar with the development of the learning process from admission to transfer?

Documenting the curriculum

1   Is the curriculum well documented?
2   Do all members of staff have their own copies?
3   Are parents able to see it?
4   Do the governors have a copy?
5   Is there a school handbook for parents?
6   Is there a staff handbook?
7   How are amendments and additions dealt with?
8   Do all members of staff undertake their planning according to
(a)   a year plan
(b)   a term plan
(c)   an action programme?

Evaluating results

1   Is the curriculum constructed to facilitate the process of evaluation?
2   Is it expressed in intended outcomes which can be assessed?
3   To what extent is record-keeping an important part of the process of evaluation?

Curriculum development

1   Is the curriculum under constant review?
2   Do I undertake an annual curriculum review?
3   Do I prepare an annual curriculum report?
4   Does it present the opportunity to
(a)   take stock
(b)   assess progress
(c)   identify new needs?

Governors

1   Does my regular report to the governors:
(a)   adequately reflect the life of the school
(b)   provide information about the curriculum
(c)   give details of current curriculum developments?

6 Spreading the load

1   What sort of authority and power system have I established in the school?
2   What is my attitude to power sharing?

3   What are the staff's attitudes to it?
4   What sorts of assumptions have I made about the staff?

Motivation

1   What is the extent of my knowledge and understanding of motivation?
2   Do I motivate by
(a)   structuring success for each member of staff
(b)   recognizing their individual contributions
(c)   helping them to derive professional satisfaction from their work
(d)   providing realistic challenges and responsibilities
(e)   providing help with career development?

Delegation

1   To what extent is delegation an essential feature of my school?
2   What sorts of decisions can children make for themselves?
3   What sorts of decisions can non-teaching staff make for themselves?
4   What sorts of decisions can teaching staff make for themselves?
5   Which functions of headship is it unthinkable for me to delegate?

The deputy head

1   What is the role of the deputy head in this school?
2   Does he have a role definition?
3   Do I regard the deputy as an active partner in the management process?
4   Is the deputy adequately prepared to take over the headship in my absence?
5   Is there a training programme for the deputy?
6   Does the training programme provide opportunities for experience and practice of the six management functions?
7   Does it provide oportunities for leadership skills and qualities to be developed?
8   How often do I meet with the deputy to consider
(a)   short-term issues
(b)   long-term issues?
9   Does the deputy have a curriculum leadership role?

Scale posts

1   Does the system of delegation
(a)   help the school to work towards clearly-defined goals
(b)   make the best use of available experience
(c)   provide support and guidance for all staff
(d)   facilitate school-based INSET and staff development
(e)   ensure continuity and progression in the curriculum?
2   How are scale posts distributed?
3   When were they last revised?
4   Do all post holders have a role definition?

5   Do all members of staff have copies of each others role definitions, including my own?

7 *Appointing staff*

1   What are the established procedures for appointments in my LEA?
2   How do I assess a staff vacancy when it arises?
3   Do the 'further details' contain all the information that a potential applicant would need?
4   Is there a systematic procedure for managing the appointment process?
5   Do I encourage potential applicants to visit the school?
6   How are the visits of potential applicants managed?
7   Do I have a strategy for dealing with applicants?
8   How do I decide the shortlist?
9   Do my letters inviting candidates contain all the information they need?
10 How is the planning for the interview undertaken? Who is involved?
11 Does everyone know about the arrangements for the interviews?
12 Is there a clear plan for the conduct of the interview?
13 Do all members of the interviewing panel have all the documents they need?
14 Are all members of the panel familiar with the details of the post on offer?
15 How is important data collected during the interview?
16 Is adequate attention given to the candidate's comfort and well-being?
17 How is the final decision arrived at?
18 How is the successful candidate informed?
19 How are the unsuccessful candidates informed?
20 How is feedback to unsuccessful candidates managed?

8 *Staff development*

1   Do I have a specific policy for staff development?
2   Are all members of staff familiar with it?
3   In attempting to identify the needs of the staff how far do I consider
(a) professional categories
(b) competence factors?
4   How far do I see my task as
(a) getting to know each teacher
(b) estimating their potential
(c) assessing their achievements
(d) bridging the gap?
5   Is the working atmosphere in the school conducive to positive staff development?
6   How far do I see staff development in terms of
(a) formal elements

(b)   informal elements?
 7   Does every member of staff have a personal file?
 8   Do I have regular appraisal interviews with each member of staff?
 9   How are staff development programmes created?
10   How are they reviewed?
11   How are programmes followed up?
12   How are whole-staff programmes managed?

9 Evaluation and accountability

1   To what extent is evaluation seen as a vital stage of the decision-making process?
2   What procedures do I have for comparing outcomes with plans?
3   Are curriculum documents constructed in such a way that evaluation is facilitated?
4   Do I use the following to assist evaluation
(a)   checklists of objectives
(b)   pupil evaluation sheets?
5   To what extent have I used the National Primary Survey to assess the work of my own school?
6   Do I use a role evaluation schedule?
7   How do I evaluate
(a)   my year plan
(b)   my term plan
(c)   my action programme?
8   How do I evaluate my leadership style?
9   To what extent do I attempt to obtain forms of external evaluation of the school?
10   How do I arrange to hear the views of
(a)   the governors
(b)   the parents
(c)   the local authority
(d)   headteacher colleagues?
11   How do I discharge my accountability to
(a)   the governing body
(b)   the local education authority?
12   What are the informal procedures of accountability?
13   To what extent do I use my regular report to the governing body to give an account of the work of the school?
14   To what extent are other members of staff involved in the accountability process?

External evaluation

The final paragraph of the Foreword to *Keeping the School Under Review* makes a most important point:

There is a danger in any form of self-assessment that people do not always see themselves as others see them. To overcome this it is hoped that schools who take into use a form of self-assessment such as is outlined in this paper will be prepared to discuss the outcomes with colleagues in the inspectorate so that they may have the benefit of an external viewpoint to put beside their own. Additionally, the possibility of some form of cross-moderation through linking at departmental or school level in relation to different aspects of assessment might be worth considering.

Fortunately there are a range of external viewpoints which a head can call upon to supplement in-school evaluation. Among the foremost of these is the school's governing body. If the governors are involved in school life and take their responsibilities seriously, then their view of the school will be one the head and staff will be anxious to consider.

Few heads decline to take seriously the attitudes of parents. There is no doubt that a school which enjoys the support of its parent body gains in confidence. This support is achieved when the head regards the public relations exercise between school and parents as one of the most important tasks. This is not a question of adopting particular policies to court popularity, but of creating a process of consultation which sets out to describe and explain the policies of the school, and which creates efficient systems for consultation. The head should always be anxious to share with parents their view of the school and to present his or her own. A high incidence of parental anxiety about the school is often an indicator of inadequate consultation.

Local authorities vary in the extent to which they wish to be involved in the process of evaluation. School inspections are sometimes carried out by the local authority and these can be very helpful to a school. Since few LEA have the resources to carry out regular evaluation by inspection an individual school is only likely to experience this form of assessment occasionally. A more positive policy is for the school to seek the help of the authority's advisory service in planning and conducting its own evaluation procedures. The adviser for primary education can be particularly helpful in the design of the process as a whole, and specialist and subject advisers in the design of its particular parts. If reports are prepared they should be constructive and specific and form the basis for useful discussions by the school's decision-making body.

Another external view which can prove very helpful is that of the head's own headteacher colleagues. It is good for heads to visit each other's schools and to work together on joint projects. There are many opportunities for cooperation and collaboration, and in the years ahead the quality of primary education may well depend upon it.

The process of accountability

The increasing demand for accountability has already been referred to. The difficulty for the head is knowing precisely how to discharge it.

While the head's authority is clearly defined in the Rules of Government for the school it becomes abundantly clear to a newly-appointed head that accountability often works not through the channels defined but directly to the local authority administration. Most of the regulations and procedures affecting schools are issued directly by the local authority and do not involve the governing body. This is particularly so in the case of finance. The governing body may be required to receive an annual audited account of the private school fund but are seldom involved in the management of capitation and other allowances. The problem that sometimes arises is knowing when to work through the governors and when directly with the education office. It is not the purpose of this book to debate the issue of governing bodies, but to point out the inevitable ambiguity that arises from a rather poorly defined relationship of school, governing body and local authority administration.

Just as it is left to heads to undertake their own role definition, so it is largely left to them to determine their own machinery for accountability. In attempting to forge a dynamic partnership between the school, the governing body and the local education authority, the head has to look for ways of making this process workable, effective and beneficial to the school.

It is important to distinguish between the informal and the formal system. The informal system operates through the development of close relationships between the school and its governors. If governors are to be familiar with the work, policies and practices of the school then they need to make regular visits. Some governing bodies arrange for their members to undertake termly visits on a rota basis. This has the advantage of involving all governors in a regular pattern of visits. But these need to be supplemented by visits with a more precise purpose, such as:

school assemblies
sports occasions
concerts and productions
awards and presentations
staff meetings
school trips and visits
work in school
appointment interviews
discussions with the head, deputy or scale-post holders
social occasions
parent/teacher functions.

All members of the governors should be on the school's circulation lists for invitations and should also receive copies of newsletters and routine notes to parents.

The formal system operates through the regular meetings of the governing body. One of the main features of these meetings is the

head's report. This should be a full and detailed account of the work of
the school since the previous meeting. Some references to this report
have already been made in Chapter 5. A list of headings under which
the report could be written might usefully include:

1 correspondence
2 staff
3 pupils
4 curriculum
5 organization
6 finance
7 site and building
8 visits and visitors
9 special events

   The correspondence heading provides an opportunity to bring to
the attention of the governors important memoranda received from
the education office as well as correspondence relating to special issues
of concern. It is under the curriculum heading that the head is able to
give details of the progress of curriculum developments since the last
meeting. Special reports on each area of the curriculum can be
included each term and these can be presented by the members of staff
with special responsibility in particular areas. The head's report of the
annual curriculum review — the results of the evaluation process —
will form the main substance of the Autumn term report. Amendments and additions to school documents should also be attached to
the report, which should always be circulated in advance of the
meeting.
   Copies of the head's report, together with the agenda and minutes
of the previous meeting, are usually circulated to key officers in the
education office. However, it is good practice to send copies of all
reports and papers to the education office. The various curriculum
reports can also be sent to the adviser with special responsibility in that
area. In addition the head should seek opportunities to discuss these
reports with advisers and officers whenever possible, for it is only by
creating good communications of this sort that the head is able to give
an account of him or herself and the work of the school.
   A successful partnership between the school, the governors and the
local authority administration will only be created and maintained if
each of these participants plays their part to the full. The governing
body and the local authority have the right to expect sound management and skilled leadership from the head, who in turn has the right to
expect good support from them.

References

DES (1977) *Education in Schools: A Consultative Document* London: HMSO

DES (1978) *Primary Education in England: A Survey by HM Inspectors of Schools* London: HMSO

DES (1980) *A View of the Curriculum* London: HMSO

DRUCKER, P.F. (1967) *The Effective Executive* London: Heinemann

GALTON, M. *et al* (1980) *Inside the Primary Classroom* London: Routledge & Kegan Paul

GALTON, M. and SIMON, B. (eds) (1980) *Progress and Performance in the Primary Classroom* London: Routledge & Kegan Paul

HARLEN, W. *et al* (1977) *Match and Mismatch – Raising Questions: Leader's Guide* Edinburgh: Oliver and Boyd

ILEA INSPECTORATE (1977) *Keeping the School Under Review* London: Inner London Education Authority

SHIPMAN, M. (1979) *In-School Evaluation* London: Heinemann Educational

Book List

In addition to the books referred to in the text the following are recommended.

COULSON, A.A., (1975) *School Administration and Management* Hull: Flag Publications
This is an inexpensive selected annotated bibliography of books about management in education.

RICHARDS, C. (ed.) (1980) *Primary Education – Issues for the Eighties* London: A & C Black
A wide-ranging selection of views about current issues in primary education.

TOWNSEND, R. (1971) *Up the Organization* London: Coronet Books
This book is not about education, but so much common sense so cheaply offered cannot be ignored.

Index